IMAGES
of Sport

CARDIFF CITY
FOOTBALL CLUB
1947-1971

European Cup-Winners' Cup glory days in the early 1970s for the Cardiff City 'matadors'.

IMAGES
of Sport

CARDIFF CITY
FOOTBALL CLUB
1947-1971

'FROM SHERWOOD TO TOSHACK'

Compiled by Richard Shepherd

TEMPUS

Acknowledgements

After the publication of my first pictorial book on *Cardiff City 1899-1947 – From Riverside to Richards*, many people asked me if there would be a sequel, so I am pleased to have been able to produce a second volume.

A number of former Cardiff City players and their relatives have contributed photographs for this book, and I am especially grateful to Robert Sherwood, son of the late Alf Sherwood, for the use of his father's photograph album. My thanks also go to the following: Fred Stansfield, Arthur Lever, Charlie Rutter, George Edwards, Ron Stitfall, Alan Harrington, Colin Baker, Derek Tapscott, Ronnie Bird, Gary Bell, Brian Clark, Gil Reece, Cardiff City director Will Dixon and long-serving Club Medical Officer Dr Leslie Hamilton, all of whom kindly allowed me to use some of their personal photographs covering their period with the Club.

Once again, my good friend Stewart Williams has allowed me the use of photographs relating to the Club from his superb *Cardiff Yesterday* series, and I would like to thank George Edwards for contributing the foreword.

I have not attempted to provide a detailed history of Cardiff City during 1947-71, but to present these photographs in chronological order to provide a reminder of players and matches in that time. I am very grateful to the Chalford Publishing Company Limited and to their Welsh editor Simon Eckley for the opportunity of producing this sequel which I hope will bring back some great memories for long-time followers of Cardiff City Football Club.

First published 1997, reprinted 2003

Tempus Publishing Limited
The Mill, Brimscombe Port,
Stroud, Gloucestershire, GL5 2QG

British Library Cataloguing in Publication Data.
A catalogue record for this book is available from the British Library.

ISBN 0 7524 0791 0

Typesetting and origination by Tempus Publishing Limited
Printed in Great Britain by Midway Colour Print, Wiltshire

Rhondda-born George Edwards, who contributes the Foreword to this book, was an outstanding left-winger with Swansea Town (1937-43), Coventry City (1943-45), Birmingham City (1945-48), Cardiff City (1948-55) and Wales (1945-49). After his retirement from playing in the mid-1950s, he became an oil company executive, a football journalist and broadcaster, and a director of Cardiff City continuously from 1957 to 1987, apart from a brief interlude. He served on the Sports Council for Wales for many years from the mid-1960s and has sat on various tribunals for the FA of Wales. He is still a major shareholder of Cardiff City Football Club and remains active in retirement in Llandaff, Cardiff. He was recently given a special Merit Award by the FA of Wales for his services to football.

Contents

Foreword

by George Edwards MA, JP

This second book of archive photographs on Cardiff City, compiled by Richard Shepherd, covers the period from 1947 to 1971 and coincides with my active involvement in the Club. Therefore, I have much pleasure in contributing this foreword.

Ninian Park is a famous footballing venue, witnessing outstanding matches with some of the greatest players in the world demonstrating their skills. We so often forget dramatic moments which occurred years ago, but this collection of photographs will help us recall some of the glorious days in Cardiff City's history, both at club and international level.

I first met Richard Shepherd long ago when he had just begun his broadcasting career. A born commentator with a natural, easy and yet exciting style, his enthusiasm for football has led him to collect a remarkable archive of old photographs, programmes, books, articles, etc. So, he is eminently placed to present this pictorial look at Cardiff City from post-war years to the early 1970s, and I, too, would like to recount a few of my own memories, both as a player and director, which these photographs have rekindled.

During the Second World War, Cardiff manager Cyril Spiers had assembled a talented group of local players – Alf Sherwood, Arthur Lever, Fred Stansfield, Billy Rees, Ken Hollyman, Bill Baker, Colin Gibson, Roy Clarke and Stan Richards, to name but a few. These were the players I eventually joined – along with Dougie Blair, Phil Joslin, Stan Montgomery and later Wilf Grant, Ken Chisholm and Trevor Ford – all of them in City teams which produced consistently good results over the immediate post-war decade.

I arrived in December 1948 from Birmingham City, but, prior to that, the Bluebirds had easily won the Division Three (South) Championship in 1946-47. So, I played against them twice in 1947-48 when Birmingham went up to Division One. We lost 2-0 at Ninian Park on 29 November 1947 in front of 42,000 in a great game, and we beat the Bluebirds 2-0 at St Andrews on Easter Saturday, 1948 to clinch promotion before a crowd of over 50,000 – a victory which ended Cardiff's promotion hopes. Little did I think, during the celebrations that day, that I would soon be a Cardiff player, and would turn the tables on Birmingham City in similar fashion a few years later!

It happened in early May 1952. Birmingham, back in Division Two, had finished their League programme and were on tour in Holland. They were in second place – only two went up then – and six points ahead of us (two points for a win). We had three games left, all at home, and a better goal average. So, all we had to do was win all three. In a tremendous eight days, with tension mounting in Cardiff and the whole of South Wales, we beat Blackburn, Bury and finally Leeds United. There were fantastic scenes after our 3-1 win over Leeds, well illustrated in this book, and Cardiff City were back in Division One for the first time since the late 1920s.

Then, in successive seasons (1952-53, 1953-54), we humbled Manchester United 4-1 and 3-2 at Old Trafford. And in that '53-54 season, we completed a 'double' over Liverpool. Our 1-0 win at Anfield put them in Division Two for eight years – heady days indeed!

My dominant memories as a director involved the second half of the 1960s when our regular winning of the Welsh Cup enabled us to create such an impact in the European Cup Winners' Cup over a seven-year period from 1964. How well I remember that last-minute goal which gave Hamburg a 1968 semi-final win at Ninian Park.

But the outstanding tie was the quarter-final against Real Madrid in March 1971 and Brian Clark's goal to give us a 1-0 home win, although Real won the return 2-0.

Richard Shepherd's delightful book has revived many precious memories for me. It will do the same for all those players and fans who remember the 1947-71 period and will also enthral current followers of the Bluebirds.

Introduction

by Richard Shepherd

For any Cardiff City fan of the immediate post-war years, i.e. the late 1940s, the one ambition was to see the Club return to the First Division of the Football League and to the status which the Bluebirds had enjoyed in the 1920s.

From the modest surroundings of Division Three (South) in 1947, City took just five years to get back to the top level. And when they did make it back to Division One, it seemed that the whole of South Wales wanted to be at Ninian Park every other week to see the likes of opponents such as Stanley Matthews, Tom Finney, Nat Lofthouse, Billy Wright – just some of the top names of British football – take on Alf Sherwood, Trevor Ford, George Edwards, etc.

An average home League attendance of just under 40,000 saw City in First Division action during 1952-53, and even by the end of the 1950s when they were back in Division Two, anything less than 20,000 at Ninian Park was considered poor!

The 1960s were modest in comparison following top-level status from 1952 to 1957, and from 1960 to 1962. But the 'Swinging Sixties' were remarkable for the Bluebirds in Europe: in 1965 they reached the quarter-finals of the Cup Winners' Cup, and the semi-finals in 1968, while 1971 saw their great quarter-final against Real Madrid.

Under manager Jimmy Scoular, the Club eventually became a force in the Second Division. In 1968-69, 1969-70 and 1970-71 they went near to regaining First Division status with Brian Clark and John Toshack providing plenty of goals. That latter season saw Toshack depart for Liverpool, but despite the arrival of the equally prolific Alan Warboys, City missed out, and have never since come close to reaching top level. That was twenty-six years ago, and this book, with some memorable photographs and match-programmes, traces City's progress 'from Sherwood to Toshack'.

The two architects of Cardiff City's post-war rise were Club Chairman Sir Herbert Merrett (left) and Secretary/Manager Cyril Spiers (below). Born in Cardiff in 1887, Herbert Merrett began his business life as an office-boy with a coal-exporting firm at Cardiff Docks, and by the mid-1930s was a major South Wales industrialist. A life-long supporter of the Club, he became a member of the Cardiff City board in March 1939, and took over as Chairman the following month. He was knighted for his services to public life in 1950, and became President of Cardiff City in 1951. He was also at one stage President of Glamorgan County Cricket Club. Sir Herbert died at the age of 72 in October 1959.

Birmingham-born Cyril Spiers was a goalkeeper with Aston Villa, Tottenham and Wolverhampton Wanderers where he was also assistant-manager. He was appointed Cardiff City manager by Sir Herbert Merrett in April 1939, and during the Second World War he ran the Club in a part-time capacity. After a contractual dispute, he left to join Norwich City in June 1946, but returned to Ninian Park in early December 1947. He remained as manager until his departure in May 1954, and was later in charge of Crystal Palace.

One
Post-War Rise
1947-1952

Pre-season training in early August 1947 as the Bluebirds prepare for their return to the Second Division after winning the Third Division (South) in 1946-47. On the sands at Coney Beach, Porthcawl, from left to right: Ken Hollyman, Ron Stitfall, Billy Baker, Danny Canning, Arthur Lever, Colin Gibson, George Wardle, Fred Stansfield, Alf Sherwood.

Skipper Fred Stansfield leads the Bluebirds out to face Chesterfield at Ninian Park in Division Two on 23 August 1947. This was the opening day of the season and 38,028 fans were there to see a 0-0 draw. Various ground improvements had seen the rebuilding of the enclosure and player's tunnel in front of the main stand. Following Stansfield out are: Arthur Lever, Colin Gibson, Alf Sherwood and Danny Canning.

Fred Stansfield shakes hands with the Chesterfield captain watched by referee Arthur Tolley of Worcester. In the background, a packed 'Bob Bank', which was to remain uncovered for another eleven years until 1958. For their return to Division Two in that '47-48 season, the Bluebirds had altered their shirt designs from all-blue to blue with white sleeves, the pattern they had worn from 1935 to 1943.

By early September 1947, City were going well, and on 8 September they defeated Southampton 5-1 at Ninian Park in front of 40,000. Here, Glyn Williams and Fred Stansfield (5) defend against Southampton's George Curtis (8) and Merthyr-born Tom Lewis.

Meanwhile off the field, City's players were encouraging young supporters, with winger George Wardle showing the boys of Cardiff Central Youth Club how it should be done. Wardle, a qualified FA coach had joined the Bluebirds from Exeter City in mid-May 1947, and went to Queens Park Rangers in late 1949.

When Cardiff City visited Chesterfield for a 2-2 draw on 20 December 1947, locally-born Ron Stitfall, normally a full-back, came in at centre-forward for the injured Stan Richards. Also in the side was Dougie Blair, signed in August 1947 from Blackpool. Son of Jimmy Blair, City's skipper of the early 1920s, Dougie was an outstanding left-side player who could appear in various positions. He was a part-timer who worked as a quantity surveyor for the Cardiff building firm John Morgan and Co. From left to right, back row: Bob Allison (trainer), Dougie Blair, Billy Baker, Danny Canning, Billy Rees, Colin Gibson, George Wardle. Front row: Ken Hollyman, Alf Sherwood, Fred Stansfield, Arthur Lever, Ron Stitfall.

No FA Cup run for Cardiff City in 1947-48 – the Bluebirds went down 2-1 to Sheffield Wednesday in the third round at Ninian Park on 10 January 1948 in front of 48,000. Here, Billy Baker tackles a Wednesday forward at the Grange End watched by Alf Sherwood (right). In the background, a packed enclosure on the Sloper Road side of the ground.

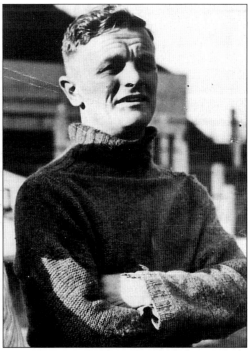

Left: Welsh internationals Alf Sherwood and Fulham winger Sid Thomas at Ninian Park, 27 March 1948, as 35,000 watch a 0-0 draw. Right: Devon-born goalkeeper Phil Joslin who was signed in July 1948 from Torquay United.

A favourite training venue for Cardiff City was the Guest Keen sports ground in Sloper Road not far from the Penarth Road junction. Several of the players are seen here in early August 1948 in front of the Guest Keen Social Club. The ground is now a private housing estate. In the group is centre-forward Bill Hullett, signed from Southern League Merthyr Tydfil in February 1948. A prolific goalscorer, Hullett went to Nottingham Forest in November 1948 and eventually returned to Merthyr as player/manager. From left to right: Fred Stansfield, Bill Hullett, Ron Stitfall, Alf Sherwood, Dougie Blair, Billy Baker, Arthur Lever, Billy Rees, Ken Hollyman.

Early '48-49 action for Phil Joslin at Ninian Park as a 40,000 crowd watches City beat Southampton 2-1. Alf Sherwood holds off Saints forward Eric Day. In the background is Ken Hollyman.

Following his £7,000 transfer from Chester, burly centre-forward Tommy Best makes his City debut in a 2-0 defeat at West Bromwich Albion on 30 October 1948. Tommy, whose nickname was 'Bull', was originally from Milford and left City for Queen's Park Rangers in December 1949. From left to right, back row: Jim Pearce (assistant trainer), Arthur Lever, Alf Sherwood, Phil Joslin, Bob Allison (trainer), Ernie Stevenson, Beriah Moore, Gordon Pembrey (reserve). Front row: Bill Hullett, Tommy Best, Fred Stansfield, Ken Hollyman, Ron Stitfall, Billy Baker.

Left: defender Stan Montgomery, signed in late November 1948 from Southend United for £6,000. Son-in-law of ex-City full-back Jimmy Nelson, Stan played for the Bluebirds until 1955. Right: Welsh international winger George Edwards arrived from Birmingham City on 11 December 1948 for £12,000. He was then studying at Birmingham University.

City began an FA Cup run with a 2-1 third round win at Oldham Athletic of Division Three (North) before a 28,591 crowd at Boundary Park, 8 January 1949. Phil Joslin blocks an Oldham shot watched by Arthur Lever.

A railway guard at Cardiff General station gives the Bluebirds the green flag for their trip to Aston Villa three weeks later for their fourth round tie. Although Alf Sherwood (left) went with the team he missed the game due to injury. A 70,718 crowd saw City win 2-1 and Villa's Welsh international Trevor Ford missed a penalty! From left to right: Alf Sherwood, Bob Allison (trainer), Phil Joslin, Ernie Stevenson, Arthur Lever, Bryn Allen, Ken Hollyman, Graham Hogg (hidden), Billy Baker, Ron Stitfall, Stan Montgomery.

Stan Montgomery leads City out for the Cup match at Villa Park. Stan had made a goal-scoring debut for the Bluebirds in a 2-2 draw at Grimsby a week earlier but had suffered a head wound which had to be protected for the game at Villa. Following Stan out are Arthur Lever, Ron Stitfall, Ernie Stevenson and Phil Joslin.

City in training at Matlock for their FA Cup fifth round tie at Derby, 12 February 1949, when the Bluebirds lost 2-1. Fred Stansfield, shown here with his team-mates, had broken his ankle a month earlier against Barnsley and never played for City again. The following season he went to Newport County where he was to become player/manager and later managed Bedford Town. He now lives in retirement in Whitchurch. From left to right, back row: Fred Stansfield, Ken Hollyman, Billy Rees, Bryn Allen, Billy Baker. Front row: Phil Joslin, Ernie Stevenson, Ron Stitfall, Arthur Lever, Stan Montgomery, Bob Allison (trainer), Alf Sherwood.

Left: inside-forward Roley Williams joined City from Milford United in early February 1949. He later played for Northampton Town and Lovells Athletic. Right: full-back Charlie Rutter (back row, left) came from Taunton Town in April 1949. An Eastender, he spent nine years at Ninian Park. He has run a pet-shop business in Cardiff Central Market for the past 35 years.

TO-DAY'S TEAMS.
(Alterations will be announced by Loudspeakers.)

RIGHT   LEFT

CARDIFF CITY 1 (0)
(Royal Blue)

MORRIS

2 STITFALL, R.   3 SHERWOOD

4 WILLIAMS, G.   5 MONTGOMERY   6 BLAIR

REES
7 BAKER   8 ~~WILLIAMS, R.~~   9 BEST   10 STEVENSON   11 EDWARDS
(1)

Referee:		Linesmen.
Mr. G. CLARK	PAGE & STIBBS EVERYTHING ELECTRICAL	Mr. A. E. BAUGHAN
(London)		Mr. G. W. PULLIN

GARREY   (1)   PATTERSON
11 ADAM   10 ~~CHISHOLM~~   9 LEE   8 KING   7 GRIFFITHS
KING   McARTHUR   SMITH
   6 ~~JOHNSON~~   5 ~~PLUMMER~~   4 ~~HARRISON, W.~~
      HARRISON   FRAME
      3 ~~SCOTT~~   2 ~~JELLY~~

BRADLEY

LEFT   RIGHT

LEICESTER CITY 1 (0)

Att. 35,000

Above, left: A 1-0 win for City at Tottenham on 5 March 1949 in front of a 51,183 White Hart Lane crowd. Stan Montgomery defends against Spurs' Welsh international skipper Ron Burgess (right) and Les Bennett.

Above, right: Bury's Dave Massart causes City a few problems during the 2-1 win on 4 April 1949. 33,000 saw the game, but again City narrowly missed out on promotion.

Left: The team-page for Cardiff City's final game of 1948-49 against FA Cup finalists Leicester City. The result was a 1-1 draw and widely believed to have been 'arranged'. Injury-hit Leicester needed a point to avoid relegation to Division Three (South) on goal average. City needed a point to finish fourth which would give the players a larger share of 'talent-money' – a bonus which the Football League allowed clubs to pay if they finished third, fourth or fifth in the division and outside the 'top two' promotion places.

Cardiff City often fielded a cricket team during summer months, and when they played a local Bridgend club in August 1949, they included three Bluebirds who were county cricketers: Stan Montgomery of Essex and Glamorgan, Ernie Carless (ex-Glamorgan) and Allan Watkins of Glamorgan and England. From left to right, back row: Roley Williams, Fred Stansfield, Elfed Evans, Stan Montgomery, Arthur Lever, Phil Joslin, Ted Gorin, Tommy Best (umpire). Front row: Ken Hollyman, Ernie Stevenson (captain), Ernie Carless, Allan Watkins, Beriah Moore.

But it was soon back to pre-season training for 1949-50. Here, Arthur Lever (right) shows his skills, watched in the background by Ken Hollyman and Fred Stansfield. Nearest the camera (left) is Alf Rowland, and (far left) is Harry May.

Alf Sherwood, George Edwards and Stan Montgomery enjoying a soak after training in August 1949. By then, George had grown a moustache which he still wears.

City had lost their opening game of the 1949-50 season 1-0 at Blackburn, but two days later on 21 August, a 40,000 crowd saw them beat Sheffield Wednesday 1-0 at Ninian Park. Here, Wednesday goalkeeper Dave McIntosh foils Tommy Best. In the background is Dougie Blair.

City's first-team in August 1949. From left to right, back row: Arthur Lever, Stan Montgomery, Phil Joslin, Glyn Williams, Ron Stitfall, Alf Rowland. Middle row: Ken Hollyman, Ernie Stevenson, Alf Sherwood, Billy Baker. On the ground: George Edwards, Roley Williams.

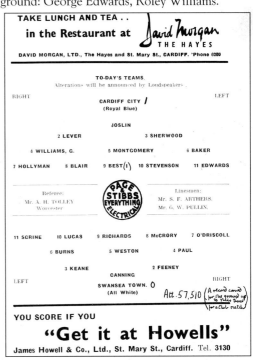

Newly promoted Swansea Town made their first League visit to Ninian Park for nineteen years in August 1949. City were 1-0 winners with a Tommy Best goal, and in the Swans line-up were ex-Bluebirds Danny Canning and Stan Richards.

A crowd of 57,510 – a League record for Ninian Park at the time – saw the game against the Swans as 'keeper Phil Joslin races out to challenge Jack O'Driscoll. Partially hidden are Billy Baker and Arthur Lever. On the right is Swansea's Frank Scrine.

The 4-2 home defeat by Leicester City on 17 September 1949 signalled the beginning of the end of Tommy Best's stay with the Bluebirds. Tommy, seen here with Leicester full-back Norman Kirkman, was injured in the game and played only one more game for City before his move to Queen's Park Rangers on 8 December 1949.

8.—In consideration of the observance by the said Player of the terms, provisions and conditions of this Agreement, the said .... *Trevor Morris* ....

.... on behalf of the Club hereby agrees that the said Club shall pay to the said Player the sum of £ ... *7 - 0 - 0* .... per week, from ... *12 September 1949* ... to ... *7th May 1950* ...

and £ ... *5 - 0 - 0* ... per week from ... *9th May 1950* ... to ... *31 July 1950* ...

9.—This Agreement shall cease and determine on ... *31st July 1950* ... unless the same shall have been previously determined in accordance with the provisions hereinbefore set forth.

(Fill in any other) *Player to be paid :-*
(provisions required.)

① Terms as per League Rule

② £1 extra when in the First Team.

As Witness the hands of the said parties the day and year aforesaid :—

Signed by the said ... *Trevor Morris* ...

and ... *C. I. Rutter* ...

In the presence of ....

Signature ... *Cyril M Spiers* ...

Occupation ... *Manager* ...

Address ... *Ninian Park* ... *Cardiff* ...

Trevor Morris,

With a maximum wage of £12 per week in League football, reserve players would be lucky to get that. These were Charlie Rutter's terms from September 1950. The contract was signed by Charlie, Secretary Trevor Morris and Manager Cyril Spiers.

Ninian Park was by now firmly established as the home of Welsh international football, and on 14 October 1949, the day prior to the Wales v England international in the Home Championship – which was also a World Cup qualifier – the Welsh team had a look at the ground. From left to right: City's Billy Baker (Wales reserve), Charlie Layfield (trainer), Trevor Ford (Aston Villa), George Edwards (Cardiff City), Cyril Sidlow (Liverpool), Ron Burgess (Tottenham). In the background between Ford and Edwards is Arthur Lever, who was not capped for Wales until he left City the following year to join Leicester.

An aerial view of Ninian Park during that Wales v England match which set a new ground record of 61,079.

City's Alf Sherwood played in that international, but despite his challenge on Jackie Milburn, the Newcastle man scored on this occasion and completed a hat-trick in England's 4-1 victory.

With no regular goal-scoring centre-forward available midway though the 1949-50 season, full-back Ron Stitfall was drafted in with some success. Here he is (between the goal posts) scoring in the 3-2 home win over Preston on 10 December 1949 on a heavy pitch. On the left are Dougie Blair and Ken Hollyman (7). Only 22,000 saw the game.

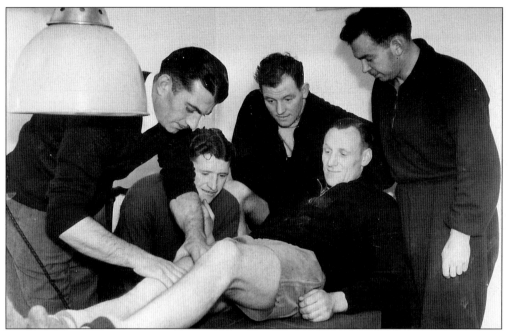

Trainer/physio Walter Robbins has a look at Stan Montgomery's knee in the Ninian Park treatment room watched by Glyn Williams, Alf Sherwood and George Edwards. Former Welsh international Robbins had been a City star in the late 1920s and early 1930s before going to West Bromwich Albion. After leaving Ninian Park in the mid-1950s, he was coach at Newport County and then Swansea.

A rare picture of two of the Stitfall brothers in a City line-up. Albert (left) closing in on the Blackburn goal at Ninian Park in a 2-1 win on 19 December 1949. Ron is next to Blackburn goalkeeper Patterson. There were in fact three Stitfall brothers at Ninian Park. Bob, a goalkeeper, never played in the first-team. Albert made several appearances before going to Torquay United in March 1952, while Ron, who joined the Club as a 15-year-old in the early 1940s, returned after war service and stayed at Ninian Park until 1965.

City's return match against Swansea Town on Christmas Eve 1949 brought them a 5-1 defeat, their heaviest that season. 'Keeper Phil Joslin, helped by Dougie Blair, clears a Swansea attack. 27,284 were at the Vetch Field.

The year ended with a 2-0 defeat against the eventual Second Division champions Tottenham Hotspur before a 59,789 White Hart Lane crowd. Phil Joslin, watched by Stan Montgomery, saves from ex-City forward Billy Rees who had joined Spurs in the summer of 1949.

Bartley Wilson, the founder of Riverside AFC which developed into Cardiff City, was still active as assistant secretary when he celebrated his 80th birthday during January 1950. Club Secretary Trevor Morris presented him with a gold pen on behalf of the staff, watched by Phil Joslin, Ron Stitfall, Arthur Lever, Billy Baker, Alf Sherwood and Ken Hollyman. Bartley Wilson retired in May 1954, while shortly afterwards Trevor Morris succeeded Cyril Spiers as manager. Trevor went to Swansea as manager in 1958.

Former City forward Billy James had been forced to give up playing in the late 1940s following his captivity by the Japanese in the Second World War, but he remained with the Club in a coaching capacity. On 1 May 1950, a 12,000 crowd attended his testimonial match between the Bluebirds and a side selected by Billy. This was City's line up, from left to right, back row: Referee, Elfed Evans, Jim Merritt (assistant trainer), Ron Stitfall, Arthur Lever, Alf Steele, Glyn Williams, Dougie Blair, Albert Stitfall, Linesman. Front row: Ken Hollyman, Billy James, Alf Sherwood, Billy Baker, Bob Lamie.

Amongst the newcomers for the 1950-51 season – when City finished third, just missing out on promotion – were half-back Bobby McLaughlin, signed from Wrexham in the summer of 1950 and winger Mike Tiddy, transferred from Torquay United in November 1950. Here they are in training at Ninian Park during that season. From left to right: Charlie Rutter, Stan Montgomery, Bobby McLaughlin, Mike Tiddy and Roley Williams.

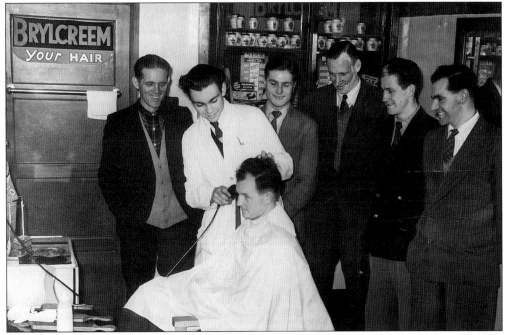

Skipper Alf Sherwood in the barber's chair during 1950-51 watched by Wilf Grant, Charlie Rutter, Stan Montgomery, Mike Tiddy and Ron Stitfall. It was during November of this season that former Southampton winger Grant, signed in March 1949, was switched to centre-forward, a move that was to help City gain promotion the following year.

In May 1951, City played two matches in the Channel Islands, winning 6-1 against Jersey and losing 2-0 to Guernsey. Here they are in Jersey enjoying a sightseeing tour. From left to right, back row: J. Atkins (supporter), Ron Stitfall, Ron Beecher (later to be a director), Cyril Spiers (manager), Tudor Steer (Chairman), Bob John (appointed assistant trainer in January 1950), Stan Montgomery, Phil Joslin, Wilf Grant, Marwood 'Mars' Marchant, Billy Baker, Channel Island FA members. Seated: Mike Tiddy, Bobby McLaughlin, Charlie Rutter, Ken Hollyman. On the ground: Elfed Evans (with camera), Derrick Sullivan.

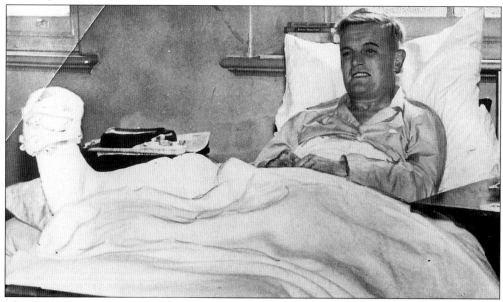

The 1951-52 season opened on a tragic note. Goalkeeper Phil Joslin broke his leg in a collision with Wilf Grant during City's pre-season public practice-match in early August 1951. Phil, shown here in St David's Hospital, never played again. City signed Welsh international Iorwerth 'Iorrie' Hughes from Luton to replace him.

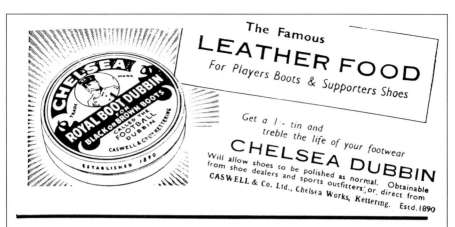
CLUB NOTES.

THIS week-end we start a new season full of hope that 1951-52 will see us pull off the promotion to the higher sphere of the First Division which we so narrowly missed last season.

On this occasion we are favoured with two home games to commence the season and should we fare as well as we did last campaign up to the vital last five games then we are much better placed as regards fixtures for of the final five matches this season four of them are at home

To talk of the end of a season while it is just starting seems brimful of wishful thinking but none are more fully aware than the Board of Directors of the possibilities of the new season now with us.

The players are all eagerly looking forward to a good season and with a fair run of the ball they are confident that the experience and understanding they have gained as a team knowing each others' play will bring the results we all expect.

PLAYERS FOR SEASON 1951-52.   In Alphabetical Order.

Goalkeepers : R. Howells, I. Hughes, P. Joslin.

Full Backs : H. Parfitt, C. Rutter, A. Sherwood, A. Stitfall, R. Stitfall, R. Thomas, E. Williams.

Half Backs : W. Baker, J. Frowen, B. Griffiths, K. Hollyman, G. Norman, R. McLaughlin, S. Montgomery, D. Moss, D. Sullivan, C. Wilcox, Glyn Williams.

Forwards : D. Blair, G. Edwards, E. Evans, L. Evans, C. Gale, G. George, W. Grant, M. Marchant, D. McCulloch, D. Mills, W. Nugent, G. Thomas, M. Tiddy, R. Williams.

Colin Gale, Emlyn Williams, Harry Parfitt and George Thomas are in H.M. Forces.

Tommy Sloan, who was one of our F.A. Cup winning team, returned to Ninian Park the other day after 21 years absence when he brought with him from Ireland Alfred Elliott, a 19 year-old centre forward, who has shown great promise as a professional with Portadown, the club Tommy manages. The old Irish international expressed amazement at the great improvements in accommodation and amenities at Ninian Park from his days as a player with the City 25 years ago.

Cardiff City's view on prospects for the 1951-52 season from the opening-day programme against Leicester City on 18 August 1951. The Club had a 34-strong professional playing staff.

The opening goal of 1951-52 as George Edwards beats Leicester 'keeper John Anderson five minutes after the start. It was City's record at home which ensured that season's success: eighteen wins, two draws and just one defeat! 35,000 saw this opening game at Ninian Park and the average crowd that season was 28,954.

Rotherham United were the only side to do the 'double' over City in 51-52, both matches in late August. In this 2-0 defeat at Millmoor on 27 August 1951, goalkeeper Iorrie Hughes takes the ball, watched by Stan Montgomery (left), Ken Hollyman and Charlie Rutter (right). This was the game in which Billy Baker unaccountably caught an innocent cross with his hands, leaving the referee with no option but to give a penalty to Rotherham.

The date is 20 October 1951, and two of British football's greatest names meet in the Wales v England 1-1 draw at Ninian Park in front of the usual 60,000. City skipper Alf Sherwood dispossesses England's legendary Tom Finney of Preston. It was one of many memorable tussles between the two during the late 1940s and '50s.

1951-52 saw full-back Charlie Rutter establish himself as City regular. He played in 30 of the 42 Second Division games. Here he is defending against Hull City in a 1-0 home win at Ninian Park on 3 November 1951. The following March, Charlie played for England B in their 1-0 win over Holland B in Amsterdam, and he became the first-ever Cardiff City player to be selected for an England representative side.

The winning goal in that victory over Hull City as Wilf Grant heads in a George Edwards centre at the Grange End. George had run practically the length of the pitch down the 'Bob Bank' touchline. Wilf Grant had a tremendous season – he scored 26 League goals plus one in the FA Cup. Oddly enough, he did not score in an away match until mid-March 1952! In May 1952, Wilf played for England B against France B.

It was Alf Sherwood's match in the 2-1 home win over Doncaster Rovers on 5 January 1952. He went off with a head wound in the first half, and while he was waiting to return, Doncaster took the lead. Alf came back to play on the right wing, scored the equaliser before half-time, and (above) scored a second-half winner!

Scottish-born forward Ken Chisholm, once of Leicester City, was signed from Coventry City in early March 1952 to boost City's attack. They lost 6-1 at Sheffield United on his debut, but when he made his first Ninian Park appearance on 14 March, he scored twice against Barnsley in a 3-0 win, and this was his first goal.

City had to win their final three games of 1951-52 (all at home) to make certain of promotion as Second Division runners-up. After beating Blackburn (3-1) and Bury (3-0), they played Leeds United on 3 May 1952 in front of a rain-soaked 51,000 crowd. Skipper Alf Sherwood spins the coin with Leeds captain Tommy Burden, watched by referee Pankhurst of Warwick. The Bluebirds had received thousands of 'good luck' messages from Welsh exiles, including many from Welsh servicemen based overseas.

CARDIFF CITY

A·F·C
·LT'D·

Official Programme

3ᴰ

SATURDAY, 3rd MAY, 1952.   Kick-off at 3.15 p.m.

FOOTBALL LEAGUE, DIVISION II.

CARDIFF CITY v. LEEDS UNITED

Registered Office and Ground : NINIAN PARK, CARDIFF.

Board of Directors :
SIR HERBERT MERRETT, J.P., *President.*
C. T. STEER, J.P., *Chairman.*   C. J. PAGE, *Deputy Chairman.*

The match-programme for the promotion-clincher against Leeds United. Club Chairman Tudor Steer, a Cardiff estate agent who had succeeded Sir Herbert Merrett in the chair, sadly died a few days after promotion was achieved.

TO-DAY'S TEAMS
(Alterations will be announced by Loudspeaker).

RIGHT   LEFT

CARDIFF CITY
(Royal Blue, White Shorts)

HOWELLS

2 WILLIAMS, G.   3 SHERWOOD

4 McLAUGHLIN   5 MONTGOMERY   6 BAKER

7 WILLIAMS, R.   8 BLAIR   9 GRANT   10 CHISHOLM   11 EDWARDS

Referee :

Mr. G. PANKHURST

(Warwick)

Linesmen :

Mr. W. J. H. OAKLEY
(Red Flag)
Mr. A. HILL
(Yellow Flag)

11 WILLIAMS   10 IGGLEDEN   9 FIDLER   8 MILLS   7 HARRISON

6 BURDEN   5 McCABE   4 KERFOOT

3 HAIR   2 MILBURN

SCOTT

LEFT   RIGHT

LEEDS UNITED

The team-page from the memorable 3-1 home win over Leeds on 3 May 1952. Wilf Grant scored twice, Ken Chisholm added another, before Leeds scored late in the game. Leeds winger Peter Harrison was later on City's training-staff while full-back Jim Milburn was Bobby Charlton's uncle.

The huge crowd see Wilf Grant (right) beat Leeds 'keeper Scott to open the scoring at the Canton End.

The final whistle has gone, and City are back in Division One. Skipper Alf Sherwood battles his way to the dressing rooms, the rest of the team are somewhere in the crowd.

City's players thank the fans for their support after the win over Leeds. On the microphone is goal-scoring hero Wilf Grant. Next to him are George Edwards, Billy Baker, Bobby McLaughlin, Ken Chisholm and Alf Sherwood.

The scene from the main stand as the fans cheer the players in the directors' box. (Inset right) Alf Sherwood, (inset, left) Club president, Sir Herbert Merrett who said to them, 'We are back where we belong, and I can assure you all that we are there to stay!'

Cardiff City's 1951-52 end-of-season squad who sealed promotion. From left to right, back row: Walter Robbins (trainer/coach), Roley Williams, Stan Montgomery, Cyril Spiers (manager), Ron Howells, Glyn Williams, Ron Stitfall, Dougie Blair. Front row: Mike Tiddy, Ken Chisholm, Bobby McLaughlin, Alf Sherwood (captain), George Edwards, Wilf Grant, Derrick Sullivan.

The Bluebirds not only made the news in '51-52, but tried their hand at reporting it as well! This photograph was taken during a two-match tour of Scotland in mid-May 1952, when they visited the Glasgow offices of Kemsley Newspapers who then owned the *Western Mail* in Cardiff. Alf Sherwood tries out the teleprinter machine watched by Mike Tiddy, Walter Robbins, Roley Williams, Stan Montgomery, teleprinter operator, Cliff Nugent and Cyril Spiers.

Two
First Division Days
1952-1957

Alf Sherwood, followed by goalkeeper Ron Howells, leads out Cardiff City at Wolverhampton Wanderers on 23 August 1952 in the Club's first Division One game since 1929. City lost 1-0, however, and then went down 3-0 at Middlesborough, Nevertheless, they managed to finish the season in mid-table. The Bluebirds' average home attendance leapt to 39,941 – the highest in their history!

Newcomers for 1952-53 included winger Keith Thomas of Sheffield Wednesday, forward Keith Norman of Aston Villa and winger George Hazlett of Bury. All three were included in the pre-season public-practice match of mid-August 1952 when the 'Whites' played the 'Blues'. Also in the line-up is 18-year-old goalkeeper Graham Vearncombe, a locally-born ex-amateur who had signed professional terms the previous season. From left to right, back row: Ron Stitfall, Harry Parfitt, Graham Vearncombe, John Frowen, Derrick Sullivan, Don Moss. Front row: Keith Thomas, Keith Norman, Cliff Nugent, Roley Williams, George Hazlett.

The newspaper reporter who covered all Cardiff City matches as football correspondent of the *Western Mail* was Dewi Lewis (left) with his familiar pipe which was always with him. Dewi, who wrote under the name 'Citizen' for many years, covered City from 1946 to 1967 when he retired. With him here is the *Western Mail*'s famous rugby correspondent, J.B.G. Thomas.

City's return to the top level attracted huge crowds on their travels, especially in London. Thousands of Bluebird fans, including many Welsh exiles, were among the 62,150 attendance at White Hart Lane on 6 September 1952 when Tottenham were 2-1 winners. From left to right: Alf Sherwood, Eddie Bailey (Spurs), Stan Montgomery, Les Medley (Spurs), Ron Stitfall and Len Duquemin (Spurs).

No health worries over cigarette advertising in the 1950s and 'Franklyn's Tobacco' was a familiar sign on the roof of the Canton Stand. The match was City against Burnley in mid-September 1952, a 0-0 draw seen by 45,100. Burnley's Doug Holden is challenged by Montgomery, watched by Sherwood (right).

43

Left: Cogan-born Alan Harrington, a former amateur who signed professional in October 1951, seen here training with George Edwards during the 1952-53 season. Right: the first Ninian Park appearance of future City manager Jimmy Scoular, on left, then of Portsmouth, playing for Scotland against Wales in October 1952.

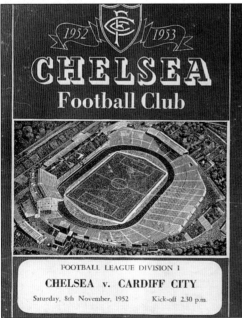

Left: City's first visit to Chelsea for twenty-two years. They won 2-0 in front of 52,132 although the victory was soured since wing-half Glyn Williams broke his leg during the game. Right: a first Wales appearance for Ron Stitfall, against England at Wembley on 12 November 1952. From left to right: Bill Short (Wales), Ray Daniel (Wales), Roy Bentley (England), Ron Stitfall (Wales).

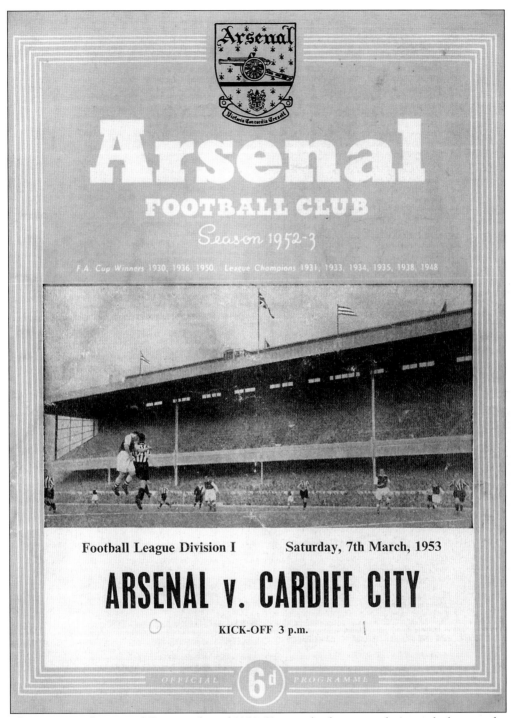

Arsenal
FOOTBALL CLUB
Season 1952-3

F.A. Cup Winners 1930, 1936, 1950. League Champions 1931, 1933, 1934, 1935, 1938, 1948

Football League Division I   Saturday, 7th March, 1953

ARSENAL v. CARDIFF CITY

KICK-OFF 3 p.m.

OFFICIAL 6ᵈ PROGRAMME

The most eagerly-awaited City matches of 1952-53 were the fixtures with Arsenal who won the League Championship that season. City had beaten them in the 1927 FA Cup final but since the late 1920s had been to the very bottom of the League and back up again.

ARSENAL 0 (0)

Goal
Kelsey

2
Right back
Wade

3
Left Back
Smith, L.

4
Right Half
Shaw

5
Centre Half
Daniel

6
Left Half
Mercer
(Capt.)

7
Outside Right
Cox

8
Inside Right
Logie

9
Centre Forward
Holton

10
Inside Left
Lishman

11
Outside Left
Roper

Referee
Mr. R. H. Mann
(Worcester)

Att 59,579

Linesmen
Red Flag
Mr. D. F. Rawlins (Herne Bay)

Yellow Flag
Mr. A. G. Joyce (Luton)

11
Outside Left
Northcott

10
Inside Left
Blair *(1)*

9
Centre Forward
Grant

8
Inside Right
Williams, R.

7
Outside Right
Tiddy

6
Left Half
~~McLauchlin~~
Sullivan

5
Centre Half
Montgomery

4
Right Half
~~Baker~~
Harrington

3
Left Back
Sherwood
(Capt.)

2
Right Back
Stitfall

Goal
Howells

CARDIFF CITY 1 (1)

The team-page from that Arsenal v Cardiff programme. Included in City's line-up is Tommy Northcott who was signed in October 1952 from Torquay United under the friendly arrangement which existed between the two clubs over transfers from the late 1940s to January 1954 when it was terminated.

Doug Blair, second from the right, about to head the only goal of the game against Arsenal at Highbury in that March 1953 meeting. City were the only side against whom the Gunners failed to score home or away that season.

Left: Doug Blair in action against Portsmouth's Len Phillips at Ninian Park in April 1953. A great individualist, Blair joined Hereford United in June 1954. Right: skipper Alf Sherwood in late 1952-53. He was regarded by then as the best full-back in Europe. He won 39 Welsh caps with City, plus one war-time cap. He was with the Club from 1942 to 1956 when he went to Newport County with whom he gained two further Welsh caps. After a spell as Barry Town player/manager, he retired in 1963. He died in March 1990 aged 66.

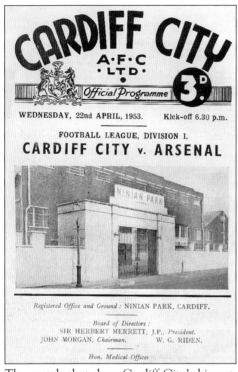

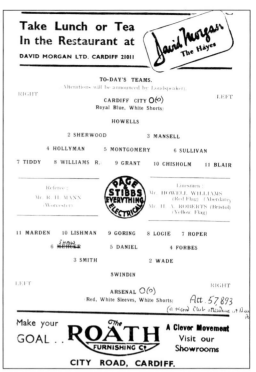

The match that drew Cardiff City's biggest-ever home attendance for a League or Cup game was this visit of First Division leaders Arsenal on 22 April 1953 when 57,893 packed into Ninian Park for a 0-0 draw. There have been bigger attendances for international matches but never as many for a club match.

The huge crowd sees Ken Chisholm (left) connect with a header at the Grange End. On the right is Arsenal 'keeper George Swindin who became City's manager from November 1962 until May 1964.

1953-54 … and City's second season back in Division One, with top names regularly in action at Ninian Park. Above: this was a 1-1 draw against Bolton on 19 September 1953 played in front of 36,000. England centre-forward Nat Lofthouse (left) heads just over the bar, watched by Stan Montgomery and Jack Mansell (3) who had come from Brighton in October 1952. Below: a week later on 26 September, and 50,000 see Arsenal win 3-0 at Ninian Park. Alan Harrington, beginning to establish himself in the team, challenges Arsenal's Jimmy Logie.

A packed 'Bob Bank' watches Wales lose 4-1 to England at Ninian Park on 10 October 1953. Leeds United's John Charles, who was to join City ten years later, leaps over England's 'keeper Gil Merrick of Birmingham City, watched by Blackpool's Harry Johnston.

The Bluebirds in white for the visit to West Bromwich Albion on 21 November 1953 when City lost 6-1! In the line-up is forward Frank Dudley who signed a month earlier from Southampton in part-exchange for Bobby McLaughlin. Dudley was soon on the move again – on 18 December 1953 he was transferred to Brentford. From left to right, back row: Doug Blair, Alan Harrington, Ron Howells, Derrick Sullivan, Billy Baker. Front row: Mike Tiddy, Frank Dudley, Stan Montgomery, Wilf Grant, Ken Chisholm, George Edwards.

Struggling Liverpool were at Ninian Park on 28 November 1953 and were easily beaten 3-1. In fact, they went down that season! Stan Montgomery, Alan Harrington and Charlie Rutter (arm raised) repel the Merseysiders' attack.

Left: a memorable encounter at Ninian Park on 31 October 1953 when Field Marshall Viscount Montgomery of Alamein met Stan Montgomery in the boardroom immediately after City's 5-0 home win over Charlton. Right: Welsh international Trevor Ford is met at Cardiff General station by BBC Welsh Region Sports Editor Alun Davies. The former Swansea and Aston Villa player had joined City from Sunderland for a League record fee of £30,000 and had made his City debut on 5 December 1953 at Sheffield Wednesday.

Trevor's home debut for City was on 12 December 1953 against Middlesborough. The attendance of 31,776 was over ten thousand up on the previous home game against Liverpool. City were 1-0 winners and here Trevor (second from left) is seen heading the only goal of the game.

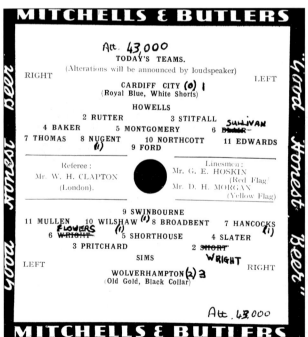

Left: top team of 1953-54 were Wolves who won the League Championship. They won 3-1 at Ninian Park on 2 January 1954 in front of 47,113. Eight internationals played in the game: Stitfall, Baker, Ford, Edwards (all for Wales); Wright, Hancocks, Wilshaw, Mullen (for England). Right: Swinbourne opens the scoring for Wales.

Charlie Rutter clears the ball during an FA Cup sensation at Ninian Park on 30 January 1954 when Port Vale, leaders of Division Three (North) won 2-0. City 'keeper Ron Howells had to be carried off unconscious after falling on the icy pitch (above). Skipper Alf Sherwood took over in goal.

FA Cup winners in 1954 were West Bromwich Albion. City beat them 2-0 in this game at Ninian Park on 10 April 1954 when the attendance was 50,967. Billy Baker (second from left) gets in a shot watched by Trevor Ford (extreme left). Baker had joined the Club from Troedyrhiw in 1938 when he was eighteen. He was captured by the Japanese during the Second World War, but returned to City in 1946 and stayed until going to Ipswich in 1955.

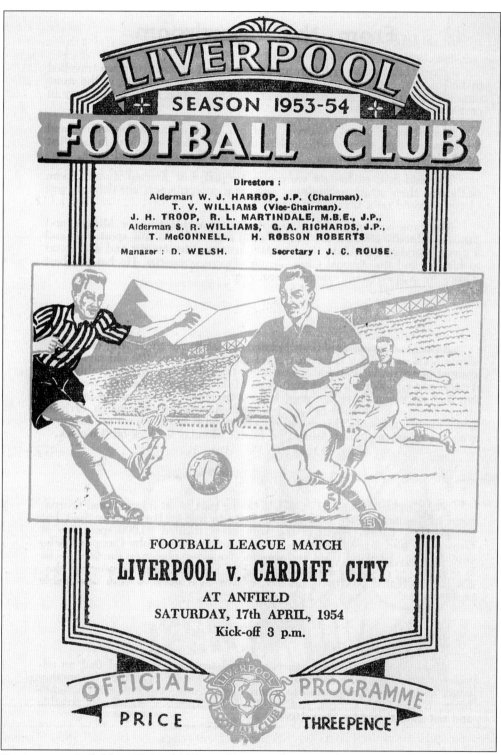

LIVERPOOL
SEASON 1953-54
FOOTBALL CLUB

Directors:
Alderman W. J. HARROP, J.P. (Chairman).
T. V. WILLIAMS (Vice-Chairman).
J. H. TROOP, R. L. MARTINDALE, M.B.E., J.P.,
Alderman S. R. WILLIAMS, G. A. RICHARDS, J.P.,
T. McCONNELL, H. ROBSON ROBERTS

Manager: D. WELSH.   Secretary: J. C. ROUSE.

FOOTBALL LEAGUE MATCH

LIVERPOOL v. CARDIFF CITY

AT ANFIELD
SATURDAY, 17th APRIL, 1954
Kick-off 3 p.m.

OFFICIAL PROGRAMME

PRICE   THREEPENCE

City's visit to Anfield on 17 April 1954, and Liverpool were on the verge of relegation from the First Division!

LIVERPOOL v. CARDIFF CITY

Right   LIVERPOOL (Red Jerseys)   Left

UNDERWOOD (1)

McNULTY (2)   LOCK (3)

G. B. WILKINSON (4)   HUGHES (5)   TWENTYMAN (5)

JACKSON(7) ANDERSON(8) SMYTH(9) EVANS(10) LIDDELL(11)

Edwards   *Grant*

GRANT(11) NORTHCOTT(10) FORD(9) NUGENT(8) ~~TIDDY~~(7)

SULLIVAN (6)   MONTGOMERY (5)   BAKER (4)

SHERWOOD (3)   STITFALL (2)

HOWELLS (1)

Left   CARDIFF CITY (Blue Jerseys)   Right

Referee : Mr. C. W. Bucknall (Birmingham).

Linesmen : Mr. W. L. Bennett (Red Flag).
Mr. J. Entwistle (Yellow Flag).

The team-page from the Liverpool v Cardiff City programme on 17 April 1954. Tommy Northcott's goal gave the Bluebirds a 1-0 win and condemned Liverpool to relegation to the Second Division for the next eight years. City 'keeper Ron Howells went off with a finger injury, Alf Sherwood took over in goal, and saved a Billy Liddell penalty!

CLUB NOTES.

THIS AFTERNOON sees the conclusion of the 1953-54 season as far as League Football is concerned and the result of to-day's game with Sheffield Wednesday can have little effect on our final position in the comfortable mid-section of the First Division table.

While we have suffered disappointments, the season on the whole, has provided evidence that the City are capable of holding their own and consolidating the foundations laid by the Directorate to firmly re-establish the Club in the First Division.

Comparison of last season's final figures, when we finished precisely in the middle of the table, with those of the present term, but *exclusive of to-day's match*, are as follows : —

		P	W	D	L	Goals F	A	Pts.
1952-53	..	42	14	12	16	54	46	40
1953-54	..	41	18	7	16	49	69	43

Satisfaction is gained in the improvement in the number of matches won this season.

Last season the City performed the " double " against but one club— Bolton Wanderers— while in this campaign a vast improvement has been shown in that we have the distinction of having beaten at home and away, Tottenham Hotspur, Aston Villa, Sheffield United, Preston North End and Liverpool, a record of achievement worthy of any club in the division and equalled by few.

* * *

In to-day's game with Sheffield Wednesday, our younger players are much in evidence. They are Graham Vearncombe (18), Allan Harrington (20), Colin Gale (21), Colin Baker (19) and Tommy Northcott (20). Tommy finishes his National Service in the Army in a few weeks time.

* * *

At Ipswich, on Monday, the Combination side picked up a valuable point in a 1 - 1 drawn game. Peter Thomas scored our goal. City XI : Jones (K) ; Thomas (R), Callan, Frowen, Hill ; Godwin, Thomas (P.), Oakley, Blair and Burder.

The Welsh League XI, in an away match at Ebbw Vale, retained their second place in the table by drawing 4 - 4. Vic Silcox (2) and Brian Rutter (2) were our scorers.

While the seniors finish their Football League matches today, the Football Combination and Welsh League sides have outstanding games to be played.

* * *

AT NINIAN PARK

Next Wednesday at Ninian Park, **BOURNEMOUTH** are our visitors in the last home fixture of the Football Combination. Kick-off 6.15 p.m.

* * *

AT CORONATION PARK

Welsh League games at Coronation Park are : —
On Monday, 26th April : Ton Pentre. Kick-off 6.30 p.m.
Thursday, 29th April : Tonyrefail. Kick-off 6.15 p.m.
Saturday, 1st May : Merthyr Tydfil. The kick-off has been arranged for 11 o'clock in the morning.

City's final game of 1953-54 was against Sheffield Wednesday at Ninian Park and this was how the match-programme viewed the season. Nineteen-year-old local boy Colin Baker made his debut in this 2-2 draw, but only 15,777 turned up, and the season's average fell to 33,000!

56

Left: Carmarthenshire-born Trevor Morris became manager in June 1954 following Cyril Spiers' departure. Trevor had become City's secretary after the Second World War. He had been a City player but injury had ended his career. He served in RAF Bomber Command during the Second World War. Right: a new programme cover for 1954-55 showing the City Hall. The Bluebirds lost this game 5-2, and lost the return a week later 7-1!

City's line-up which lost 7-1 at Preston on 1 September 1954. From left to right, back row: Charlie Rutter, Roley Williams, John Frowen, Graham Vearncombe, Mike Tiddy, Billy Baker. Front row: Tommy Northcott, Alan Harrington, Alf Sherwood, George Edwards, Wilf Grant.

Following their FA third round exit at Arsenal, the Bluebirds had to fill their vacant fourth round date with a home 'friendly' against Second Division Fulham who won 2-1 at Ninian Park. Fulham's Bedford Jezzard (left) heads towards goal watched by a young Bobby Robson (8), later to become England manager. Between them is City's 19-year-old Islwyn Jones, while on the right are Alan Harrington and Derrick Sullivan. During the 1954-55 and 1955-56 seasons, the Bluebirds played in blue shirts with white sleeves.

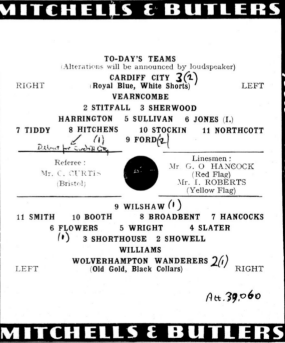

Forward Gerry Hitchens was signed from Kidderminster for £1,500 in January 1955. He later played for Aston Villa, Inter Milan, Cagliari and England. Gerry made a goal-scoring City debut on 30 April 1955 against Wolves, when the Bluebirds won 3-2 to escape relegation (right).

58

City's third goal in the 3-2 relegation escape against Wolves. A packed 'Bob Bank' sees Trevor Ford (hidden behind England player Billy Wright) beat Wolves' England 'keeper Bert Williams.

Amongst the newcomers for 1955-56 was Johnny McSeveney from Sunderland. Harry Kirtley and Howard Sheppeard also came with him from the North-East club.

'Blues' against 'Whites', in the final public practice-match of mid-August 1955. Above: the Blues line-up. From left to right, back row: Harry Kirtley, Mike Tiddy, John Frowen, Ron Howells, Alan Harrington, Islwyn Jones. Front row: Ron Davies, Ron Stockin, Charlie Rutter, John McSeveney, Gerry Hitchens. Below: the Whites line-up. Back row: Cecil Dixon, Rhys Thomas, Dennis Callan, Graham Vearncombe, Cliff Nugent, Tommy Bevan. Front row: Colin Baker, Idris Niblett, Roley Williams, Colin Gale, Howard Sheppeard.

The 1955-56 season opened promisingly with a 3-1 home win over Sunderland seen by 36,000. Here, Ron Stockin, signed from Wolves in September 1954, sees his effort blocked by Sunderland 'keeper Willie Fraser on 20 August 1955.

Things soon began to go wrong, however, and when Wolves came for this game on 3 September 1955, the 42,060 crowd was stunned as City went down 9-1! Johnny McSeveney breaks though, watched by Alan Harrington (left). In the background are Alf Sherwood and Derrick Sullivan.

This was City at Bolton a week later, losing 4-0. From left to right, back row: Charlie Rutter, Gerry Hitchens, Ron Howells, Alan Harrington, Ron Davies, Johnny McSeveney. Front row: Cecil Dixon, Harry Kirtley, Derrick Sullivan, Islwyn Jones, Roley Williams.

Two of British football's greatest names meet in Cardiff's Royal Hotel as City's Alf Sherwood calls in to renew his acquaintanceship with Stan (later Sir Stanley) Matthews of Blackpool. This was a few days before Wales played England at Ninian Park in October 1955. Sherwood and Matthews only played against each other twice at Ninian Park – both times in 1955-56 when Wales beat England 2-1, and Cardiff City defeated Blackpool 1-0.

Left: on 8 December 1955, Cardiff City signed centre-half Danny Malloy from Dundee for £17,000. He was a Scottish League cap who became a 'B' international during his five years with City. Two days after his arrival, he and locally-born Neil O'Halloran (right) made their debuts against Charlton. Here O'Halloran is pictured leaving the pitch after the game, in which he scored a hat-trick. He later became Chairman of Barry Town.

Welsh international John Charles (right) challenges Ron Howells in the Leeds v Cardiff City FA Cup third round tie at Elland Road on 7 January 1956. Danny Malloy is on the left. City won 2-1, and a year later in 1957 won 2-1 at Elland Road again in round three. Amazingly, the two clubs met yet again at Elland Road in January 1958 in the third round, and again City won 2-1 – a remarkable sequence.

After narrowly avoiding relegation, City reached the Welsh Cup final, beating Swansea Town 3-2 at Ninian Park on 30 April 1956 to win the trophy for the first time since 1930. A Welsh Cup record crowd of 37,500 saw the game. Here, the two captains – Trevor Ford of City and Ivor Allchurch of Swansea – meet at the kick-off. The referee is Mervyn Griffiths of Newport who had officiated in the famous Blackpool v Bolton FA Cup final in 1953.

A fearsome shoulder-charge by Trevor Ford on Swansea 'keeper Johnny King during that Welsh Cup final. Trevor was well-known for his 'solid' challenges which were perfectly legal in those days. On the right is Gerry Hitchens.

Johnny McSeveney heads past Johnny King to put City two up in the 1956 Welsh Cup final. The Bluebirds had dropped the white sleeves from their shirts in October 1955.

Trevor Ford receives the Welsh Cup in the directors' box from FA of Wales President Milwyn Jenkins. On the left is FAW Secretary Herbert Powell.

Derrick Sullivan takes a celebratory drink from the Welsh Cup in the dressing-room. Included in the team was winger Brian Walsh signed from Arsenal in September 1955, but absent from the group is Harry Kirtley who broke his leg in the game and was detained in hospital. From left to right, back row: Harrington, Vearncombe, Hitchens. Front row: Stitfall, Sullivan, Malloy, McSeveney, Colin Baker, Walsh and Ford.

City players were always welcome visitors to the Victoria Club in Canton. This was a 1956 presentation by club members to popular Cardiff featherweight Gordon Blakey (front). Next to him is Wales' former World Flyweight champion Jimmy Wilde. From left to right, back row: McSeveney, Kirtley, Ford, Victoria Club manager Bill Geach, Sherwood and Welsh entertainer Stan Stennett.

Trevor Ford (left) was appointed City's captain following the departure of Alf Sherwood to Newport County in the summer of 1956. And by now Colin Baker (right) was firmly established in City's line-up. He had made his City debut two years earlier, succeeding namesake Billy Baker.

By mid-September 1956, City were beginning to slide. This was the team which lost 2-1 at Birmingham City on 22 September. From left to right, back row: Ron Stitfall, Alan Harrington, Graham Vearncombe, Ron Davies, Neil O'Halloran. Front row: Danny Malloy, John McSeveney, Trevor Ford, Gerry Hitchens, Cliff Nugent, Derrick Sullivan.

Left: inside-forward Brayley Reynolds, signed from Lovells Athletic for £2,500 in May 1956, stayed two years at Ninian Park before joining Swansea Town. Right: a new programme design saw its debut on 29 September 1956 showing Ninian Park as it was in the 1950s before the 'Bob Bank' was covered.

High-flyer Graham Vearncombe in action at Tottenham on 13 October 1956, but City lost this one 5-0. Also shown are Ron Davies (next to Vearncombe), Danny Malloy (background) and Alan Harrington. On the left is Spurs' Welsh international Terry Medwin. Cardiff-born Vearncombe was with City from 1952 until 1964.

Left: former City skipper Alf Sherwood was back at Ninian Park on 20 October 1956 to lead Wales against Scotland in a 2-2 draw. Here he is meeting referee Bob Mann (Worcester). Right: a rare injury for Sherwood during that game. City skipper Trevor Ford watches anxiously as Bluebirds' trainer Bob John helps. All three were very much part of the Wales set-up at international level.

A packed Grange End in the background, with two great names at Ninian Park in that Wales–Scotland match: John Charles of Leeds United (right) and Scotland captain George Young of Rangers.

Another FA Cup third round trip to Leeds, and for the second consecutive year, white-shirted City win 2-1. Graham Vearncombe takes the ball from John Charles. Colin Baker (left) and Derrick Sullivan (6) look on. In the background is Ron Stockin.

It was relegation from Division One for City at the end of 1956-57, and a 3-0 home defeat by Tottenham on 20 April 1957 didn't help. Johnny McSeveney missed this penalty in that game against Spurs 'keeper Ron Reynolds. McSeveney left the Club that summer to join Newport County.

Soon after going down, City appointed their former winger and Welsh international George Edwards as a director. Here he is at his first board meeting in May 1957. From left to right: Fred Dewey, Sir Herbert Merrett (President), Ron Beecher (Chairman), Trevor Morris (Secretary/Manager) and George Edwards.

Three
A Brief Relegation
1957-1960

The 1957-58 season began with three new forwards in the team: Colin Hudson from Newport County, Ron Hewitt from Wrexham and England international Johnny Nicholls from West Bromwich Albion. This was the first-team that played the reserves in the final public-practice match in mid-August 1957. From left to right, back row: Rutter, Sullivan, Harrington, Vearncombe, Hitchens, Stitfall. Front row: Hudson, Hewitt, Malloy (captain), Nicholls, Nugent.

A local derby to start the new season with a 43,000 crowd watching City draw 0-0 with Swansea Town at Ninian Park. At the top of the 'Bob Bank' is the hospital broadcast box. Here, Gerry Hitchens gets in a header with help of Johnny Nicholls, watched by Ron Hewitt (8) and Ken Tucker (far right). Ken is now Chairman of the FA of Wales Senior International Committee.

Left: Joe Bonson was signed from Wolves for £10,000 in early November 1957 as City struggled to make an impact in the Second Division. He was to be a regular goal-scorer during his three years with the Club. Right: the departure of Gerry Hitchens, for a Club record fee of £22,000 to Aston Villa just before Christmas 1957, did not go down well with City fans. Here he is in his final City appearance on 14 December 1957 at Fulham in a 2-0 defeat. The Fulham 'keeper is Tony Macedo.

74

Early January 1958, and the Bluebirds leave Ninian Park for a third consecutive FA Cup third round tie at Leeds, which once again they win 2-1. From left to right: Ken Jones, Brayley Reynolds, Ron Hewitt, Cliff Nugent, Alec Milne, Danny Malloy, Colin Baker, Joe Bonson, Alan Harrington, Ron Stitfall, Ron Beecher (Chairman), Trevor Morris (manager), John Evans (physio), Nat Kahn (supporter). In the doorway of the coach are Brian Walsh and Derrick Sullivan.

A comfortable 4-1 win for City against Leyton Orient in round four of the FA Cup, and a big crowd of 35,849. But 'keeper Ken Jones can't prevent an equaliser for Orient. Also shown are Alan Harrington (4), Danny Malloy and Alec Milne (3).

Two Cardiff City players took part in Wales' 2-0 home-leg win over Israel at Ninian Park in a World Cup qualifying play-off on 5 February 1958 – Ron Hewitt, winning his first cap, and Alan Harrington. Wales qualified for the finals in Sweden that summer, with Hewitt, Colin Baker and Derrick Sullivan all in their squad. From left to right, back row: Alan Harrington, Stuart Williams, John Charles, Jack Kelsey, Mel Hopkins, Ivor Allchurch, Mel Charles. Front row: Terry Medwin, Ron Hewitt, Dave Bowen, Cliff Jones.

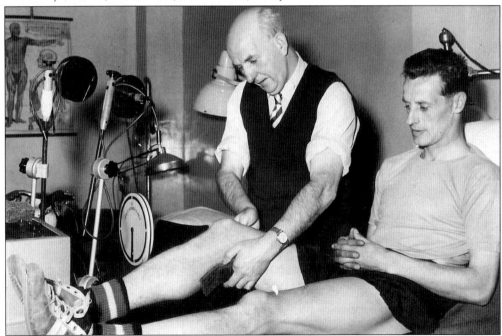

Bluebirds winger Brian Walsh under treatment at Ninian Park from City physio John Evans in 1958. Following his transfer from Arsenal in September 1955, Walsh was with City until 1961 when he joined Newport County. He qualified as an accountant during his time with Cardiff.

The Manchester United air disaster at Munich in early February 1958 had an effect on everyone on football. In common with all other clubs, there was a minute's silence two days later before the Cardiff City–Doncaster Rovers match at Ninian Park on 8 February. The referee is Ken Aston. Nearest the camera, on the right, is Colin Hudson. In the Doncaster line-up (second from left) is centre-half Charlie Williams, later to become a famous comedian.

The Bluebirds in playing formation on the day before they met Blackburn Rovers at home in the FA Cup fifth round on 15 February 1958. From top: Ken Jones, Alec Milne, Ron Stitfall; Alan Harrington, Danny Malloy, Colin Baker; Brian Walsh, Ron Hewitt, Joe Bonson, Cliff Nugent, Colin Hudson.

City's fifth round FA Cup tie against Blackburn was the last time they would progress this far in the Cup for another fourteen years! 45,580 saw a 0-0 drew against the Lancashire club, City losing the replay 2-1. Goalkeeper Ken Jones punches clear with Alec Milne (2) in support. On the right are Danny Malloy and Alan Harrington.

Early April 1958, and a disappointing season approaches its end. Bristol City come to Ninian Park on Easter Friday (4 April) and win 3-2. Joe Bonson (left) and Ron Hewitt (right) watch opposing 'keeper Bob Anderson gather the ball. The other Bristol City player is skipper Tommy Burden. This was one of the last pictures of the open 'Bob Bank'. In the summer of 1958, a large cover was built, which remains to the present day.

Above, left: Club Coach Bill Jones, who had come to Ninian Park from Worcester City in the summer of 1957, was appointed acting-manager in July 1958 after the departure of Trevor Morris to Swansea Town. A former Barry boss, Jones became permanent manager in October 1958 until his departure in September 1962. Above, right: November 1958 saw the return of Wilf Grant to Ninian Park. City's former centre-forward came from Llanelli as trainer/coach. He had left Ninian Park to join Ipswich in 1955, and was to stay with City until September 1962 when he left together with Bill Jones.

Newcomers to City's professional staff in the summer of 1958 included 17-year-old Hengoed-born Graham Moore. He scored a last-minute equaliser on his City debut in a 2-2 draw at Brighton, in mid-September 1958. He made the score-sheet on his Wales debut with a last-minute equaliser against England at Ninian Park in October 1959, and he scored City's promotion-winning goal against Aston Villa in April 1960.

In those days of a maximum wage in League football, clubs carried large playing staffs. Cardiff City had thirty-nine professionals at the start of 1958-59 and pictured here is the line-up which played the first-team in the pre-season public-practice on 16 August 1958. From left to right, back row: George McGuckin, Graham Moore, John Griffin, Alex Gray, Terry Owen, Ron Hill, Ross Menzies. Front row: Jackie McMillan, Cliff Nugent, Brayley Reynolds, Brian Jenkins.

Welsh international inside-forward Derek Tapscott joined Cardiff City from Arsenal for a modest £10,000 in mid-September 1958. The former Barry Town player, shown here in Arsenal action against Spurs' Ted Ditchburn, had been with the London club for nearly five years, and rejoined his old Barry manager Bill Jones at Cardiff.

Despite City's Second Division status, Ninian Park continued to be the home of Welsh international matches. Scotland won 3-0 on 18 October 1958 with the usual 60,000 attendance, many of whom were able to take advantage of the new cover over the 'Bob Bank'. Here Scotland's 'keeper Bill Brown (Tottenham) clears from Blackburn's Roy Vernon (8). Denis Law, then with Huddersfield, made his international debut in this game.

November 1958 saw the departure of Cliff Nugent to Mansfield. He had joined City from Headington (now Oxford) United in February 1951, and had been one of the Bluebirds' best utility players, able to appear on either flank or at inside-forward.

Derek Tapscott's form for City earned him a recall to the Welsh international team. Here he is (right) having scored for Wales in the 2-2 draw against England at Villa Park on 26 November 1958. Immediately behind him is England captain Billy Wright.

Railway travel was the usual method of transport to away matches. A happy-looking City team leave for their FA Cup fourth round tie at Norwich in mid-January 1959. They weren't too happy on the way back, however, as Third Division Norwich won 3-2 and went on to reach the semi-finals. In the window, from left to right are: Walsh, Baker and Reynolds. On the platform: Milne, Sullivan, Malloy, Jenkins, Stitfall, Tapscott, Hewitt, Milne.

Left: at the end of '58-59, goalkeeper Graham Vearncombe was back in the team, with regular choice Ron Nicholls returning to county cricket with Gloucestershire. Graham had been in dispute with City, and re-signed in February 1959 after spending four months in the Merchant Navy. Right: City reached the Welsh Cup final in April 1959, and played Lovells Athletic, the Newport confectionery manufacturers' team, at Somerton Park, Newport. Former City star Roley Williams was a van-driver with the firm and played against his old club.

The Cardiff City line-up which beat Lovells 2-0. Colin Hudson captained the team since the match was played at his old club Newport County, and he scored City's second goal. Joe Bonson got the other. From left to right, back row: Alec Milne, Steve Gammon, Graham Moore, Graham Vearncombe, Danny Malloy, Colin Baker. Front row: Brian Walsh, Derek Tapscott, Colin Hudson, Joe Bonson, Ron Stitfall.

This was the heading of an article early in the 1959-60 season which saw City win promotion back into Division One. And this was how the main stand appeared from Sloper Road after the Second World War up to 1973 when the extension to the stand was completed.

City's first-team face the camera in the Grandstand Club bar in August 1959. Two newcomers are in the group: winger John Watkins from Bristol City, and forward Steve 'Kalamazoo' Mokone from Dutch club Heracles. From left to right, back row: Bonson, Milne, Nicholls, Vearncombe, Baker, Sullivan, Stitfall. Middle row: Walsh, Tapscott, Malloy, Moore, Watkins. Front row: Harry Knowles, Harrington, Mokone, Alan Durban, Hudson.

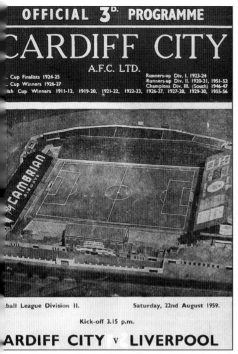

OFFICIAL **3**ᴰ· PROGRAMME

CARDIFF CITY
A.F.C. LTD.

.. Cup Finalists 1924-25
.. Cup Winners 1926-27
lsh Cup Winners 1911-12, 1919-20, 1921-22, 1922-23,

Runners-up Div. I. 1923-24
Runners-up Div. II. 1920-21, 1951-52
Champions Div. III. (South) 1946-47
1926-27, 1927-28, 1929-30, 1955-56

:ball League Division II.   Saturday, 22nd August 1959.

Kick-off 3.15 p.m.

ARDIFF CITY v LIVERPOOL

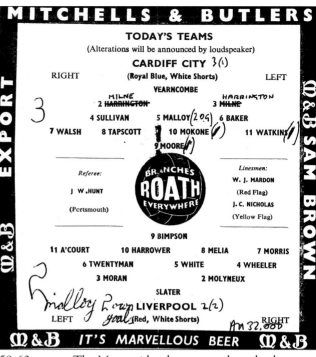

MITCHELLS & BUTLERS

EXPORT M&B

TODAY'S TEAMS
(Alterations will be announced by loudspeaker)

CARDIFF CITY 3(1)
(Royal Blue, White Shorts)

RIGHT   LEFT

YEARNCOMBE

3

2 ~~HARRINGTON~~ MILNE   3 ~~MILNE~~ HARRINGTON

4 SULLIVAN   5 MALLOY(2 og)   6 BAKER

7 WALSH   8 TAPSCOTT   10 MOKONE (✓)   11 WATKINS (✓)

9 MOORE (✓)

Referee: Linesmen:

J W .HUNT   W. J. MARDON

(Portsmouth)   (Red Flag)

ROATH
BRANCHES EVERYWHERE

J. C. NICHOLAS

(Yellow Flag)

9 BIMPSON

11 A'COURT   10 HARROWER   8 MELIA   7 MORRIS

6 TWENTYMAN   5 WHITE   4 WHEELER

3 MORAN   2 MOLYNEUX

SLATER

LEFT   LIVERPOOL 2(2)
(Red, White Shorts)

RIGHT

An 32,000

M&B   IT'S MARVELLOUS BEER   M&B

M&B SAM BROWN

City v Liverpool on the opening day of 1959-60 season. The Merseysiders have never been back to Ninian Park since! A 32,000 crowd saw City win 3-2 and score all five! Two own-goals by Danny Malloy put Liverpool 2-1 up at half-time. Mokone, Moore and Watkins scored for City.

The Bluebirds were amongst the pacemakers from the start. Derrick Sullivan scores in the 2-0 home win over Derby County on 16 September 1959. One of City's greatest servants, 'Ginger' Sullivan joined the Club from Temple Street YMCA in Newport near the end of 1947 when he was seventeen. He could play in various positions, and became a Welsh international. He left City for Exeter in the summer of 1960.

Derek Tapscott scored 21 League goals in that 1959-60 promotion season. Here are two of them. Above: a header in the 5-1 home win over Leyton Orient on 10 October 1959. In the background, the main stand as it used to be. Below: a diving effort to open the score in a 4-4 home draw against Stoke City on 21 November.

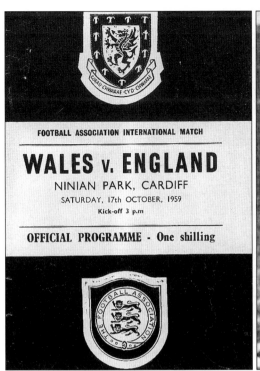

Graham Moore's international debut was in the 1-1 draw at Ninian Park for which 61,711 tickets were sold, with the official crowd recorded as just over 60,000. And here is Graham (above right) heading Wales' last-minute equaliser. Below left: the top two met in December 1959 when Aston Villa beat City 2-0 in front of 54,763. Below right: Villa's former Bluebird Gerry Hitchens beats Danny Malloy in the match.

It was a good year all round for the Club – City's reserves won promotion to Division One of the Football Combination. Here they are mid-way through the 1959-60 season. From left to right, back row: Alex Gray, Ron Nicholls, Alan Durban, Mike Hughes, Bob John (trainer). Middle row: Steve Mokone, Alan Harrington, Harry Knowles, Brian Jenkins. Front row: Colin Hudson, Barrie Hole, Alan Monk.

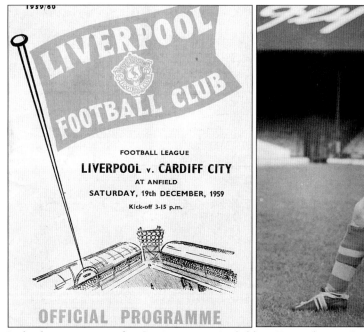

Left: the programme for City's visit to Anfield in December 1959. It was Bill Shankly's first game in charge – City won 4-0! Right: Brian Walsh had many fine games for City, but none better than in that 4-0 win at Liverpool when he destroyed the Merseyside defence.

CARDIFF CITY
A.F.C. LTD.

F.A. Cup Finalists 1924-25	Runners-up Div. I. 1923-24
F.A. Cup Winners 1926-27	Runners-up Div. II. 1920-21, 1951-52
Welsh Cup Winners 1911-12, 1919-20, 1921-22, 1922-23, 1926-27, 1927-28, 1929-30, 1955-56, 1958-59	Champions Div. III. (South) 1946-47

Football League Division II.   Saturday, 16th April 1960
Kick-off 3.15 p.m.

CARDIFF CITY v ASTON VILLA

GOLDEN JUBILEE   *Official programme* 6D

The programme for the City–Villa game on Easter Saturday, 1960. The Club had been incorporated as a professional football company in April 1910, fifty years earlier, and Aston Villa had played the first match at Ninian Park the following September. City won this game against the Second Division leaders to go back to Division One.

The goal which took Cardiff City back into Division One. Graham Moore volleys in a Colin Hudson centre to give the Bluebirds a 1-0 win over Villa. The attendance was 55,000 – the biggest in the country that day. City played in their 'lucky' white strip.

Celebrations at the final whistle with Alec Milne (left) and skipper Danny Malloy. Above Milne's head in the crowd is Colin Baker. The police officer facing the camera is Canton-based Sgt. Harry Perks, a familiar figure at Ninian Park for many years.

Four

A Short Stay in Division One 1960-1962

Peter Donnelly of Scunthorpe United was one of four newcomers in the summer of 1960. He came in part-exchange for Joe Bonson. Peter is shown here in action at Fulham on the opening day of the season.

The start of 1960-61, and Graham Moore heads City's second goal in the 2-2 draw at Fulham on 20 August. The Craven Cottage crowd was 30,995!

Left: Graham Vearncombe saves from Arsenal's Geoff Strong at Ninian Park on 24 September 1960. City won 1-0, and the 35,000 crowd saw Derek Tapscott, playing against his old club, score the winner with his hand! Right: England 'B' winger Derek Hogg was signed from West Bromwich Albion for £12,000 in late October 1960. He stayed until the end of 1961-62.

City's FA Cup third round tie against Manchester City in January 1961 went to a second replay at Highbury before the Bluebirds went out. This was the first game at Ninian Park with Danny Malloy (white shirt) defending. City's goalkeeper is Maurice Swan, signed that summer from Drumcondra in Ireland.

Left: Cardiff City's record first-team win was 16-0 against Knighton Town in the Welsh Cup on 28 January 1961. The scorers were Tapscott (6), Moore (4), Walsh (2), Donnelly (2), Malloy (1), Hogg (1). Right: Welsh international forward Dai Ward came from Bristol Rovers for £11,000 in February 1961. However, he did not get a regular place until the following season.

A memorable occasion when Tottenham Hotspur came to Ninian Park on their way to a League and Cup 'double' in 1960-61. The match was played on a Saturday night following the Wales–Ireland Rugby international at the Arms Park. Many rugby followers were amongst the 45,580 crowd who saw City come from behind to win 3-2 (Hogg, Walsh, Tapscott). But the Bluebirds didn't win another game to the end of the season!

94

City's 'keeper Ron Nicholls punches clear against Tottenham, with Danny Malloy in support. Dave Mackay of Spurs is on the right, Bobby Smith (left) watches. It was Nicholls' last season with City and he continued to be Gloucestershire's opening batsman for a number of years.

Trouble at the Grange End in that game against Tottenham as tension mounts. Alan Harrington has to separate Graham Moore and Dave Mackay. On the left are Malloy and Stitfall. On the far right is the late John White, one of Spurs' greatest players.

Ninian Park at the start of 1961-62 when the all-time ground record attendance was set. There were just 5,500 seats in the Grandstand and Canton Stand in a capacity of 60,000. The floodlights were erected in the summer of 1960.

Two new names were in Cardiff City's early-season line-up in 1961–62: forward Johnny King from Stoke City and locally-born Frank Rankmore who stepped up from the reserves to replace Danny Malloy who had gone to Doncaster. This was the side at Sheffield United in late August 1961. From left to right, back row: Colin Baker, Barrie Hole, Frank Rankmore, Graham Vearncombe, Alec Milne. Front row: Brian Walsh, Johnny King, Dai Ward, Alan Harrington (captain), Graham Moore, Derek Hogg.

City's performances for the first three months of 1961–62 were quite good, and they were unlucky to lose this game 3-2 at Tottenham in early September. Graham Vearncombe and Colin Baker are pictured here defending at White Hart Lane. In the background are Bobby Smith, Frank Rankmore and Cliff Jones.

October 1961 – three Bluebirds sign in at Porthcawl's Seabank Hotel, joining up with the Wales team to face England at Ninian Park a few days later. Dai Ward, Alan Harrington and Colin Baker (Welsh reserve) are met by Aston Villa's Phil Woosman.

The game which drew Ninian Park's record attendance of 61,566 – Wales 1 England 1 on 14 October 1961. From left to right: Stuart Williams (Wales), John Charles (Wales), Jack Kelsey (Wales), Bobby Charlton (England), Alan Harrington (Wales), with Ray Pointer (England) behind him, Mel Charles (Wales), on the ground.

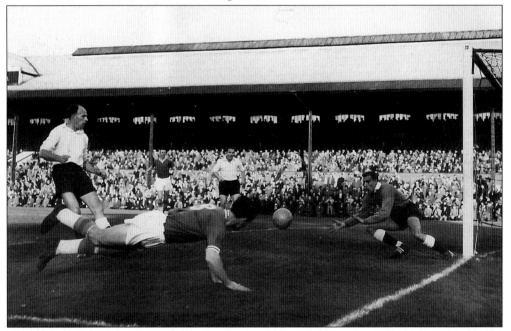

Derek Tapscott dives in to head City's winner in the 1-0 victory at Fulham on 4 November 1961. The Bluebirds didn't win another League game away from home in 1961–62 and gained just four more victories in Division One that season.

Labour Party leader Hugh Gaitskell (in coat) visited Ninian Park on 25 November 1961 for the Cardiff City v Ipswich Town match. From left to right: John Cobbold (Ipswich Chairman), Fred Dewey (City director), Ron Beecher (City Chairman), Hugh Gaitskell, Sir Edward Williams (Wales Labour Party), George Edwards (City director).

One of England's greatest goal scorers – Jimmy Greaves – in action for Tottenham at Ninian Park on 13 January 1962. But on this occasion he was robbed by Alan Harrington (left). Graham Vearncombe is City's 'keeper, and Cliff Jones is in the background. The crowd was 34,020 and City drew 1-1.

During mid-February 1962, Cardiff City signed Wales and former Swansea Town player Mel Charles from Arsenal for £20,000. Mel, younger brother of John Charles, is seen here in the Bluebirds first-team squad soon after his arrival. From left to right, back row: Tapscott, Hogg, Hole, Rankmore, John, Vearncombe, Durban, Charles, Johnny King, Milne. Front row: Ward, Danny McCarthy, Peter King, Harrington, Baker, Tony Pickrell, Trevor Edwards.

City's time in Division One is running out. This was one of West Ham's goals in the Bluebirds 4-1 defeat at Upton Park on 20 April 1962. Dilwyn John, Frank Rankmore and Colin Baker can only watch helplessly. There were now just four games left for City and despite two wins, they went down.

Five

The Second Division
and Europe
1962-1968

One of Welsh football's greatest names
came home in the summer of 1962 when
City signed Wales and Newcastle United's
Ivor Allchurch for £20,000. The ex-
Swansea Town player made his Bluebirds
debut on 18 August 1962 against his former
club Newcastle at Ninian Park, and here he
is in action during an exciting 4-4 draw in
front of 27,673.

There were managerial changes at Ninian Park during the early part of 1962–63. Bill Jones and coach Wilf Grant were sacked in early September. Former Arsenal goalkeeper George Swindin of Norwich City was appointed manager at the start of December. Here he is (on the left) that month with long-serving trainer Ernie Curtis, and ex-City defender Stan Montgomery whom Swindin had brought in from Norwich City soon after his arrival. They are seen here supervising a training session opposite Ninian Park.

City's first-team in late April 1963. Hard-shooting outside-left Peter Hooper, signed from Bristol Rovers for £10,000 in the summer of 1962, scored 24 League and Cup goals in his one season with the Club. From left to right, back row: Trevor Peck, Gareth Williams, Frank Rankmore, Dilwyn John, Mel Charles, Colin Baker, Alan Harrington. Front row: Trevor Edwards, Alan McIntosh, Derek Tapscott, Ivor Allchurch, Peter Hooper. In the background is the old press box which later became 'Radio Ninian'.

It's August 1963, and the great John Charles of Leeds, Juventus, Leeds (again) and Roma is in Cardiff's Royal Hotel to met City directors Fred Dewey (left) and Chairman Ron Beecher shortly before Charles signed for the Bluebirds for £20,000. Next to John is Italian agent Gigi Peronace, and the late Tom Lyons of the *Daily Mirror* who covered City's matches for many years.

John Charles' first appearance for City was in the mid-August 1963 public practice-match. On the right are Stitfall and Edwards. In the opening game, Charles scored with a 75-yard indirect free-kick which went in off Norwich 'keeper Kevin Keelan's shoulder.

The photograph of the late Sir Herbert Merrett looks down on a Cardiff City board meeting in 1963–64. From left to right: Viv Dewey, Fred Dewey (Chairman), George Edwards, Bob Williams.

April 1964, a month after skilful winger Greg Farrell came from Birmingham City. Scottish youngster Don Murray and local boy Peter Rodrigues are establishing themselves in the team. This group contained five Welsh internationals, apart from Tapscott, Baker and Stitfall. From left to right, back row: Gareth Williams, Barrie Hole (international), Don Murray, John Charles (int.), Mel Charles (int.) Trevor Peck, Steve Gammon (under-23 int.). Front row: Dick Scott, Greg Farrell, Dilwyn John, Graham Vearncombe (int.), Ivor Allchurch (int.), Peter Rodrigues.

Jimmy Scoular was appointed Cardiff City manager in June 1964 in succession to George Swindin. The photograph shows Jimmy with his wife Joyce and youngest daughter on their arrival at Ninian Park. The former Portsmouth, Newcastle and Scotland wing-half had been player/manager at Bradford Park Avenue, and was to have a nine-year stay with the Bluebirds.

Scoular always led from the front. Here he is taking an early '64–65 training session at Coronation Park, not far from the ground.

1964–65 was 35-year-old Ivor Allchurch's last season with City, but he was still good enough to retain his Welsh international place. Here he is in Bluebirds action against Bolton at Ninian Park in early September 1964. Bolton won, as usual. Also shown are Dick Scott (ex-Norwich) and Tommy Halliday, signed from Dunbarton in October 1963.

City had their first experience of the European Cup Winners' Cup in 1964–65. They beat Esbjerg and holders Sporting Lisbon before losing to Real Zaragoza. Here, they are off to Spain for the first leg of their quarter-final. From left to right: Peter King, John Charles, Lew Clayton (trainer), Jimmy Scoular, Gareth Williams, Derek Tapscott, Bob Wilson, Bernard Lewis, Peter Rodrigues, Alan Harrington, George Johnston, Graham Coldrick, Keith Ellis, Lyn Davies, Don Murray, Graham Keenor (Secretary), Ivor Allchurch.

The final City appearance by Ivor Allchurch was in this Welsh Cup final play-off against Wrexham at Shrewsbury on 5 March 1965. City won 3-0, Allchurch scoring twice, and they were in Europe again. From left to right, back row: Don Murray, Graham Coldrick, Bob Wilson, John Charles, Barrie Hole, Colin Baker, Ivor Allchurch. Front row: Peter King, Gareth Williams, George Johnston, Bernard Lewis.

Left: Irishman Terry Harkin was signed from Crewe on 12 August 1965. Here he is in a pre-season friendly with Hereford United a few days later. Right: sixteen-year-old local boy John Toshack, shown here with John Charles shortly after Toshack because an apprentice-professional at the start of 1965–66.

With City's squad needing to be rebuilt, Barrie Hole (left) was eventually sold to Blackburn at the end of '65–66 for £40,000. Peter Rodrigues had gone to Leicester City for £40,000 in late December 1965. This is Hole in action against Leyton Orient at Ninian Park on 13 November 1965. Bob Wilson is on the right. John Toshack made a scoring debut as substitute in this 3-1 win.

Full-back Bobby Ferguson was signed from Derby County in late December 1965 for £4,000. Here he is in the City line-up which was to beat Port Vale 2-1 in an FA Cup third round match in late January 1966. Ninian Park was snowbound at the time. From left to right, back row: Baker, Williams, Hole, Davies, Murray, Ferguson. Front row: Farrell, Johnston, King, Harkin, Lewis.

Winger Ronnie Bird is welcomed to Ninian Park by manager Jimmy Scoular after his £7,000 move from Bury in early February 1966. Ronnie and Jimmy had played together at Bradford Park Avenue when the former Scottish international was player/manager there.

There was a dramatic end to the 1965–66 season. With three games left, City played Middlesborough at Ninian Park – the winner would stay up, the loser would go down. City won 5-3 and winger Greg Farrell played the game of his life. Barrie Hole (left) scores City's opener.

Former England amateur international forward Bobby Brown cost £10,000 from Northampton Town in October 1966 as Cardiff City again flirted with relegation. Here's Brown coming out at Ninian Park on 18 February 1967 against Manchester City in the FA Cup fourth round. Behind him are Bird, Coldrick, Ferguson and Murray.

The Bluebirds draw 1-1 with Manchester City on a heavy pitch in front of 37,205. Above: skipper Gareth Williams hits the equaliser. But they lost the replay at Maine Road. Wembley-born Williams left for Bolton in October 1967.

The 1967–68 Cardiff City squad shown before the start of a memorable European Cup Winners' Cup season. Dave Carver had come from Rotherham in January 1966; Brian Harris was signed from Everton in October 1966 and Norman Dean from Southampton in March 1967. From left to right, back row: Norman Dean, Bobby Ferguson, Lyn Davies, Bob Wilson, John Toshack, Derek Ryder, Dave Carver. Front row: Bernard Lewis, Graham Coldrick, Brian Harris, Gareth Williams, Peter King, Bobby Brown, Ronnie Bird, David Summerhayes.

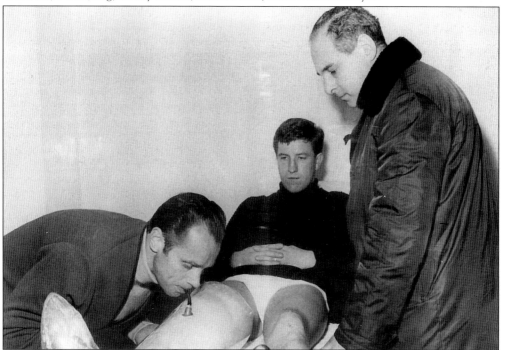

Tragedy struck Bobby Brown on Boxing Day 1967 in the 3-0 home win over Aston Villa. He suffered a badly dislocated knee and his playing career was finished. He's seen here shortly afterwards with a revolutionary new plastic splint being inflated by trainer/coach Lew Clayton. Watching is long-serving Club Medical Officer Dr Leslie Hamilton who joined the Club in August 1965 and is still there.

Left: signed in December 1967 from Blackpool for £20,000, Les Lea became part of a good City team in the late 1960s. He went to Barnsley in the summer of 1970. Right: there was no more popular player at Ninian Park at that time than Brian Clark, signed from Huddersfield for £10,000 in February 1968 to replace the unfortunate Bobby Brown.

City reached the semi-finals of the European Cup Winners' Cup in '67–68 after beating Shamrock Rovers (Ireland), NAC Breda (Holland) and Moscow Torpedo (USSR). Here, City and Torpedo line up on 6 March 1968 before the start of the home quarter-final which the Bluebirds won 1-0 with a Barrie Jones header.

The second leg against Torpedo involved a marathon trip to Tashkent in Soviet Central Asia, and an 8,000-mile round trip! The Bluebirds party is pictured in Tashkent in festive mood. From left to right, back row: Jack Haines (supporter), Bryn Jones, Malcolm Clarke, Sandy Allan, Dr Leslie Hamilton (medical officer), John Toshack, Leighton Phillips, Bill O'Donovan (supporter), George Edwards (director), Gary Bell, Jimmy Scoular (manager), Steve Derrett, Viv Dewey (director). Middle row: Bobby Ferguson, Brian Harris, Lyn Davies, Bob Wilson, Ronnie Bird, Peter King. Front row: Don Murray, Norman Dean, Lew Clayton (trainer/coach), Barrie Jones, 'Taff' Jones (supporter).

СОСТАВЫ КОМАНД

(ориентировочно)

„КАРДИФФ-СИТИ" (Уэльс)	„ТОРПЕДО" (Москва)
1. Боб Уилсон	1. Анзор Кавазашвили
2. Грехэм Голдрик	2. Александр Чумаков
3. Боб Фергюссон	3. Леонид Пахомов
4. Малкольм Кларк	4. Владимир Сараев
5. Дан Мюррей	5. **Виктор Шустиков**
6. Бобби Браун	(капитан команды)
7. **Брайан Харрис** (капитан команды)	6. Владимир Бреднев
	7. Виктор Алексеев
8. Барри Джонс	8. Владимир Щербаков
9. Питер Кинг	9. Эдуард Стрельцов
10. Джон Тошек	10. Александр Ленёв
11. Рон Бёрд	11. Давид Паис
Старший тренер—**Джимми Скулер**	Начальник команды—мастер

The team-page of the Moscow Torpedo v Cardiff City programme in Tashkent on 19 March 1968. The Bluebirds lost 1-0, but won the play-off 1-0 in Augsberg, Germany. The City line-up is on the left: 1. Bob Wilson, 2. Steve Derrett, 3. Bobby Ferguson, 4. Malcolm Clarke, 5. Don Murray, 6. Brian Harris, 7. Brian Jones, 8. Norman Dean, 9. Peter King, 10. John Toshack, 11. Ronnie Bird. Manager: Jimmy Scoular.

Seven year-old City fan David Collins from Barry came dressed for the part to see off his heroes at Cardiff Central station for their semi-final first-leg trip to HSV Hamburg in late April 1968. From left to right: Les Lea, Don Murray, Richie Morgan, Bob Wilson, Bobby Ferguson, Peter King, John Toshack, Ronnie Bird, Dave Carver, Norman Dean, Brian Harris, Malcolm Clarke. Not shown in this photograph, but also with the group were Barrie Jones, Lyn Davies, Bryn Jones, Steve Derrett. City came back with a 1-1 draw.

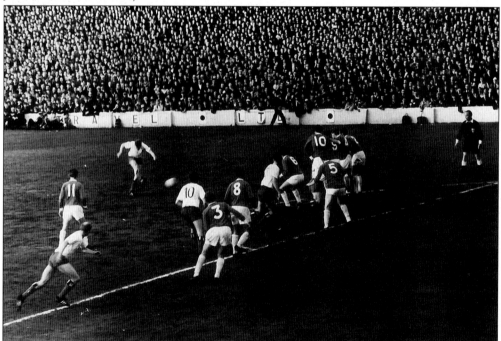

But the dream ended on 1 May 1968 when 43,070 saw City lose 3-2 with the last kick of the game. Here, no fewer than nine Bluebirds defend against a Hamburg free-kick.

114

Six

Three Near-Promotion Efforts and Real Madrid 1968-1971

City undertook a fourteen-match tour of New Zealand and Australia from late May until early July 1968. This was in Perth with Les Lea, Brian Clark and Dave Carver getting their eye in for the new season.

Sightseeing in Perth, Western Australia, in early July 1968 are Norman Dean, Graham Coldrick, Barrie Jones and Ronnie Bird.

Back at Ninian Park after the tour 'down under', manager Jimmy Scoular looks concerned about the season ahead. Good luck to the youngsters wanting autographs. In the background is Richie Morgan.

1968–69 was the year that the Brian Clark–John Toshack goal-scoring partnership really took off as City mounted a promotion challenge. Here, Clark is pictured heading City's opener in a 5-1 win at Fulham on 7 December 1968. Fulham's goalkeeper is Ian Seymour.

The Bluebirds' biggest home League crowd for five years – 22,424 – saw a 2-0 win over promotion challengers Millwall a week later, and City were now joint second. Brian Clark heads the ball to John Toshack (right) who scored City's first late in the game.

A familiar sight for Cardiff City fans – the old Ninian Park pub on the corner of Leckwith Road and Wellington Street a few hundred yards from the ground. It was eventually demolished in 1978.

An elderly gentleman visits his old school to share his memories with the children. Seventy-five-year-old Fred Keenor, captain of City's 1927 FA Cup-winning team against Arsenal, called at Stacey Road Junior School in early January 1969 shortly before City played Arsenal in an FA Cup third round tie.

Left: Graham Keenor, son of City's famous ex-captain, was City's Secretary from 1959 until November 1972. Graham had originally joined the Club as a young player in the early 1950s. Right: Welsh international winger Barrie Jones, signed from Plymouth in March 1967, was switched to midfield in October 1968, with great success. However, he broke his leg in October 1969, and his career was over.

Don Murray leads out City to face Arsenal at Ninian Park in the FA Cup third round on 4 January 1969. City were second in Division Two, Arsenal third in Division One. Behind Don are Brian Clark, Barrie Jones, Dave Carver, Steve Derrett, Gary Bell and Ronnie Bird.

Brian Clark (8) and John Toshack battle it out with Arsenal's Peter Simpson and Ian Ure (left). A crowd of 55,136 at Ninian Park saw a 0-0 draw and there were 52,000 at Highbury when Arsenal won the replay 2-0, one of the goals coming Bobby Gould, now Wales manager.

Watching from the bench against Arsenal – Brian Harris (refilling his pipe), Bobby Brown and Jimmy Scoular. On the right is Spencer Kemp, well known in local football circles and a hard-working volunteer behind the scenes for the Bluebirds.

A bone-hard pitch as Brian Clark scores at the Canton End in a 5-0 home win over Oxford United on 8 February 1969. It was one of the few games played that day, and was the main game on *Match of the Day*. Above Clark's left arm is Ron Atkinson. But City's promotion challenge faded at the end.

Cardiff City were now a major force in Division Two. This was the first-team squad in August 1969. From left to right, back row: Les Lea, Peter King, Frank Sharp, Dave Carver, Brian Clark, Leighton Phillips, Jimmy Scoular (manager). Front row: John Toshack, Barrie Jones, Ronnie Bird, Don Murray, Sandy Allan, Gary Bell, Steve Derrett.

Left: Brian Harris was a valuable member of City's defence in the late 1960s. He shown here at Sheffield United in mid-September 1969 with Graham Coldrick (right) and Don Murray (5). Between them is Cardiff-born Gil Reece. Right: Peter King was still going strong in 1969. He joined City from Worcester in 1960 and stayed until 1974. Here he is in action against Queen's Park Rangers in late September 1969. Behind him is Rodney Marsh.

Gary Bell, signed as a winger from Lower Gornal in February 1966 for just £750, was switched to full-back with great success in 1968. This was against QPR in September 1969 when 30,083 saw City win 4-2. The referee is A.E. Morrisey of Cheshire.

Scottish under-23 international Don Murray had by now developed into an outstanding defender with the Bluebirds, as this tackle on QPR's Rodney Marsh illustrates.

Bobby Woodruff, a skilful midfield player noted for his massive throw-ins, was signed from Crystal Palace in November for £20,000. Here he is on his City debut against Preston at Ninian Park on 22 November 1969.

'Manager of the month' for December 1969 after a run of seven consecutive League and Cup wins to the turn of the year, Jimmy Scoular receives his award. However, City again narrowly missed out on promotion in 1969-70.

Left: major newcomer for 1970-71 was former Scottish under-23 midfielder Ian Gibson who cost £35,000 from Coventry City. He is seen here at Ninian Park against Hull City on 31 October 1970. On the left is Hull player/manager Terry Neill. Right: the 5-1 home win over Hull was John Toshack's last City appearance at Ninian Park and he scored a hat-trick! Eleven days later, after winning at QPR to go third in Division Two, City sold Toshack to Liverpool for £110,000.

Left: Alan Warboys arrived from Sheffield Wednesday six weeks later on Christmas Eve for £45,000 – he proved a good goalscorer, including all four in a 4-0 win over Carlisle in March 1971. Right: local boy John Parsons, son of City's kit-manager Harry Parsons, broke into the first-team as a substitute during February 1971 and scored four goals in his first four League and Cup matches.

City's line-up for the 1-0 home win over Oxford United on 6 February 1971 at a time when the Bluebirds were strong candidates for promotion and in the quarter-final of the European Cup Winners' Cup. From left to right, back row: Brian Harris, Gary Bell, Mel Sutton, Jim Eadie, Dave Carver, Brian Clark, John Parsons. Front row: Peter King, Ian Gibson, Don Murray, Leighton Phillips, Nigel Rees.

Brian Clark's famous goal from a Nigel Rees cross against Real Madrid which gave City a 1-0 first-leg home win over the Spanish Cup holders in front of 47,500. It was the quarter-final of the European Cup Winners' Cup.

A training-session at the Bernabeu Stadium before the second leg against Real Madrid. Several thousand Spaniards turned up to see City going through their paces.

City, however, lost the return leg 2-0 in an ill-tempered game. Leighton Phillips and Don Murray show Czech referee Karol Soska a broken bottle which had been thrown from the crowd at Gary Bell (on the ground).

Meanwhile in Division Two, City's promotion efforts began to falter. Brian Clark (left) heads over Watford's bar in a costly 1-0 home defeat on 17 April 1971. The Watford players are Tom Walley (now with the FA of Wales) and 'keeper Mike Walker (now Norwich manager). On the right is Alan Warboys.

Three games left, and City have to win at promotion-favourites Sheffield United. But the Bluebirds lose 5-1 in front of 42,963 – John Flynn heads United's second past Jim Eadie. Others, from left to right: Steve Derrett, Brian Clark, Gil Reece, Dave Carver. City miss out for the third year – they have never come close since then, and their average home attendance of 21,609 has never been approached by succeeding City sides.

Twenty-five years on, and several of Cardiff City's 1970-71 team meet up again at an FA of Wales awards ceremony in September 1996. From left to right, back row: Gary Bell, Brian Clark, Bobby Woodruff, Leighton Phillips, Don Murray. Front row: Ronnie Bird, Peter King, Ian Gibson.